Creative
Glass
Techniques

Creative Glass Techniques

FUSING
PAINTING
LAMPWORK

BETTINA EBERLE

Lark Books
Asheville, North Carolina

For Markus, Seraina, and Gian-Andrea

Special thanks go to my husband, my co-workers Edeltraud and Susanne, my father, and Susi and Claudia for their support. I also wish to thank the firms Cerdec AG, Keramische Farben, Frankfurt/Main, and Michel Keramikbedarf, Zurich, for their fine cooperation.

Photography:
   Susi Müller, Frauenfeld, Switzerland

Design and composition:
   Mühlberg Atelier, Basel, Switzerland: Birgit Blohmann

Translation from the German:
   Mary Killough

Cover Design:
   Chris Bryant

Published by Lark Books
50 College Street
Asheville, NC 28801, USA

Originally published as Bettina Eberle, *Faszination Glas: Ein Arbeitsbuch fur Glass Fusing, Glasmalerei und Flammenarbeit mit Glas*, Verlag Paul Haupt (Berne, Stuttgart, Wien), 1997

©1997 by Paul Haupt Publishers, CH-Berne

English translation ©1997, Lark Books

Library of Congress Cataloging-in-Publication Data
   Eberle, Bettina.
      [Faszination Glas. English]
      Creative glass techniques : fusing, painting, lampwork / by Bettina Eberle.
         p. cm.
      Includes bibliographical references and index.
      ISBN 1-887374-30-2
      1. Glass craft. 2. Glass fusing. 3. Glass painting and staining. 4. Glass blowing and working. I. Title
   TT298.E2313   1997
   748—dc21   96-53011
                                                               CIP

10 9 8 7 6 5 4 3

Distributed in the U.S. and Canada by Random House, Inc.

The written instructions, photographs, designs, patterns, and projects in this volume are intended for the personal use of the reader and may be reproduced for that purpose only. Any other use, especially commercial use, is forbidden under law without written permission of the copyright holder.

Every effort has been made to ensure that all information in this book is accurate. However, due to differing conditions, tools, and individual skills, the publisher cannot be responsible for any injuries, losses, or other damages that may result from the use of the information in this book.

(Working with glass involves risks. Before using equipment or paints, read the instructions for use and follow all safety rules. The publisher works from the premises that all statements and recommendations concerning procedures and techniques are correct, but the author, the owner of the copyright, and the publisher cannot assume liability for damages.)

Printed in Italy

ISBN 1-887374-30-2

Table of Contents

Lampwork

Troubleshooting   **148**

Glass, glass
What is that?
It is and is not,
It is light and no light,
It is air and not air,
It is fragrance without fragrance,
And still it is hard,
Unseen hard presence,
To the captured bird, who does not see it
And whom it draws into the distance.
I want to create a song of glass,
To devise a hymn
In the spirit deep inside dry moisture,
Glass, glass
What is that?
It gleams like water and is not wet.
Pour water in a glass
Clear and pure:
It becomes glass in glass,
And it is wine,
Then the glass is full of color and fragrance,
And the glass itself is nothing or air:
A shape from air, a shape from nothing,
An empty, luminous child of light.
Where are you glass? I do not see you,
Only the ray which is refracted in you.
Perhaps you are a parable of the spirit,
A mirror fed by images and rays.
Spirit has neither time nor place
And is nonetheless the treasure of all treasures.

Excerpt from Gerhart Hauptmann's "The Harvest of Corn"

Introduction

✧ ✧ ✧

Thoughts about This Book

There is hardly a better answer to the question "What is glass?" than the poem by Gerhart Hauptmann on page 7. Several years ago I became interested in glass as a material, and today the many possibilities of shaping it fill my days. With this book, I would like to share my fascination and bring other people closer to the working material that is glass, inspiring them to discover beauty, distinction, and harmony in glass work.

During my many years as a teacher at home and abroad, I always urged my students to enjoy their own ideas to the fullest and to create freely. I was often asked where I got all my ideas. No general, valid recipe for inspiration exists, but certainly one must open one's eyes and senses. Many impressions, events, and experiences can be transformed into individual and personal creations that carry the clear signature of the creator. I find that making a simple sketch or jotting down a couple of key words can often help capture ideas as they occur. The complete concept can be recorded on paper at home. This way I always have a supply of ideas.

I believe that all people have the capacity—indeed the need—to express themselves artistically in some manner. What a wonderful balance for our often all-too-hectic daily lives! Let us take the opportunity to develop this capacity, using glass as our material. Make unusual glass creations with the help of my book. Realize your desire to actually do so. Stick to your own ideas, even if they turn out to be difficult to achieve in the beginning. Creative ideas are free, and their possibilities are almost limitless.

This book is intended to convey the technical principles necessary to transform your ideas into your own creations in a correct manner. For this purpose, I will introduce you to three different techniques: glass fusing, glass painting, and lampwork. These techniques all have very special design possibilities, and they can also be combined, as several of the projects demonstrate. Common to them all, however, is the fascinating basic material—glass.

❱ *Glass Fusing*

The first section of this book covers the basic uses of the glass-fusing technique—that is, melting pieces of glass together and then shaping them. The projects in this section provide a survey of this fantastic handicraft, one practiced since the days of ancient Egypt. Several of these projects also serve as the basis for projects in the second section of this book, on glass painting.

❱ *Glass Painting*

Glass painting and its countless possibilities are given special attention here. You'll learn a variety of techniques and how to apply them effectively. Probably the most familiar forms of glass painting are those on church windows and coats of arms, as well as the silk-screen printing on drinking glasses (company logos or product symbols).

All of the projects in this section are everyday objects that you can enjoy using at home and that will also be very welcome as gifts. Unfortunately, glass painting is not a very well-known creative activity, but these projects will certainly make it new friends.

❱ *Lampwork*

We will touch only lightly on this topic, because propane gas and oxygen are necessary for proper lampwork, and in order to use these substances correctly, you would need a thick book on that subject alone. We'll therefore limit ourselves to work that can be done safely with a multipurpose torch: making glass beads for jewelry by using glass sticks and glass rods, and reshaping existing drinking glasses.

Individual techniques are covered extensively in their corresponding sections. Precise descriptions of the technical procedures required to make the projects are accompanied by many photos designed to clarify the steps involved. The projects cover the greatest possible variety of procedures.

Make use of all this information to design your own creations. Have fun working with glass and good luck!

What is Glass?

The Chemical Composition of Glass

❭ *Soda-Lime Silica Glass*

Soda-lime silica glass, the most common type of glass, consists of silica (silicon dioxide), soda, and lime (calcium oxide). Bottles, canning jars, simple drinking glasses, and so on, are made from this material. Because it is more light permeable than any other available glass, soda-lime silica glass is also used to make windows.

❭ *Lead Crystal Glass*

Lead crystal glass consists of silica, lead oxide, soda, and potash. Because this type of glass has a very high capacity for refracting light, it is ideal for cut-glass work. Fine drinking glasses, vases, and decorative items are usually made from this type of glass. The lead in it—a dissolved lead oxide—is a stable ingredient that is not released when used in drinking glasses.

❭ *Borosilicate Glass*

Borosilicate glass, which consists of silica, boron dioxide, soda, and potash, is very resistant to chemicals and very insensitive to temperature variations. This glass is used mainly in the chemical industry and for making ampules, medicine containers, light bulbs, and oven-proof dishes. Craft glassblowers also use borosilicate glass as their primary material.

❭ *Special Glass*

Included in this category are optical glass, glass conductors for electronic uses, and glass for medical uses (X-ray glass and X-ray glass plates). Each of these types of glass is made according to a special recipe and for a specific purpose.

Methods of Producing Glass

All glass is created in the same way. The ingredients are mixed well and melted together in a furnace. A flux (one of the best known is sodium oxide) is added to the mixture in order to speed up the melting process by lowering the melting point.

❭ *Flat Glass*

- Glass sheets, blown or machine-made
- Float glass, produced by floating molten glass on molten tin (see page 13)
- Cast glass, poured and pressed. Glass with a wire-mesh inlay is one example.

❭ *Hollow Glass*

- Blown glass (glasses, vases, etc.)
- Machine-blown glass (bottles, standard glasses, etc.)

12 **Methods of Shaping and Working with Glass**

❱ *Glassblowing*

The raw materials for lampworkers—glass tubes and rods—are shaped over a flame produced with a gas mixture of propane and oxygen. Lampworkers work at temperatures of about 2550°F (1400°C), shaping the hot glass with metal or graphite tools, which don't adhere when they're applied briefly to the soft, glowing yellow glass. Glassblowers, on the other hand, first use a blowpipe to remove a gob of glass from the kiln at temperatures ranging from 2200°F to 2550°F (1200°C to 1400°C). They then blow through the pipe to make the most astounding objects. To shape the glass, they usually use wet wooden forms. The moisture in the hot glass disperses into the wood, and the steam, which forms a layer between the wood and glass, prevents the glass from sticking to or burning the wooden form.

❱ *Glass Casting*

In this technique, the liquid glass is taken from the furnace, poured into a form, and usually pressed as well. The glass temperatures are between 2200°F and 2550°F (1200°C and 1400°C).

❱ *Glass Fusing*

Glass fusing (melting pieces of glass together) is executed in an electric kiln at temperatures ranging from 1470°F to 1650°F (800°C to 900°C). During the firing, several sheets of glass are fused together. The glass becomes soft but does not liquify during this procedure.

❱ *Making Cut Glass*

Lead crystal glass is often cut. Because glass is a very hard material, special polishing materials and diamond-coated tools are used for this purpose.

❱ *Glass Engraving*

Designs are engraved into the glass with a small, diamond-covered instrument.

❱ *Glass Painting*

Glass paint, mixed with a special oil, is applied to the glass and fired onto it at about 1040°F (560°C).

Methods of Industrial Production

❯ *Glassblowing*

In a computer-controlled operation, the exact amount of glass is drawn from the furnace, brought to a blowing apparatus, and blown, with a specific amount of air pressure, into a mold. Coca-Cola bottles are made in this fashion.

❯ *Glass Casting*

Float glass, from which most window glass is made, is obtained by floating molten glass on a bath of molten tin inside a furnace. The viscous glass is poured (or floated) onto the molten tin and rolled to the desired thickness; the tin bath guarantees absolutely flat glass surfaces. Window glass used to be made by drawing the glass through roller devices that left marks on the glass surfaces. These surface irregularities are now avoided by allowing the glass to float on the tin.

❯ *Glass Pressing*

A small amount of molten glass is emptied into a mold, and a counter-piece is pressed on top of it. This production method renders glass pieces in many different shapes and makes it possible to produce a large number of pieces rapidly.

Coloring Various Types of Glass

In order to obtain colored glass, given amounts of metal oxides are mixed in with the other ingredients before they are melted. To make opaque glass, fluoride is also added as a clouding agent. The chart below will give you some idea of the color nuances that metal oxides make possible.

METAL OXIDE	COLOR
Cobalt oxide	Light to dark blue
Copper oxide	Blue-green
Silver compounds	Yellow
Uranium oxide	Greenish-yellow
Iron oxide	Green
Selenium	Rose to orange
Gold	Ruby red to rose
Manganese dioxide	Burgundy red

Glass Fusing

What is Glass Fusing?

Glass fusing is the process of joining pieces of glass by melting them together. These days, the term "glass fusing" often refers to an additional step, that of shaping the fused pieces. The goal of fusing itself is to produce a solid glass sheet from individual pieces of glass that are arranged beside or on top of one another and then melted together in a kiln. This first step is called "full-fuse firing." In a second step, the fused piece is then shaped, again in a kiln, to make an object such as a bowl. For shaping glass, a variety of molds, into which the glass pieces can be "slumped" or over which they can be "sagged," are required.

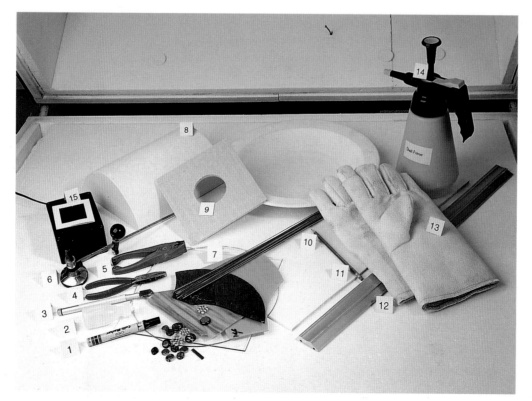

Photo 1

1. *Waterproof felt-tip pen*
2. *Glass cutting oil*
3. *Glass cutter*
4. *Grozing pliers*
5. *Breaking pliers*
6. *Circle cutter*
7. *Glass*
8. *Ceramic (or metal) molds*
9. *Ceramic fiberboard molds*
10. *Ceramic fiber sheets*
11. *Pencil*
12. *Metal ruler*
13. *Heat-proof gloves*
14. *Shelf primer*
15. *Stressometer (or strain viewer)*

Equipment and Materials

❱ *Waterproof Felt-Tip Pen*

This is the type of pen best suited for marking on glass. The waterproof colors are easily removed with mineral spirits.

❱ *Glass Cutting Oil*

You will need this oil, which is available from glass suppliers, to protect your glass cutter and to ensure perfect scoring of your glass. You'll apply a bit of oil at the beginning of the line to be scored and then draw the cutter smoothly from that point.

❱ *Glass Cutter*

This is your most important tool! Good scoring is a prerequisite for breaking glass neatly. For the best scoring, be sure to purchase a very good cutter with an oil reservoir. When you aren't using the cutter, keep it standing upright in a container with a bit of cutting oil in it.

❱ *Grozing Pliers*

Grozing pliers are used to nibble off very small pieces of glass remaining along the edges of scored and broken glass (a process known as "grozing"). They're also ideal for breaking off narrow strips of glass.

❱ *Breaking Pliers*

Breaking pliers are a practical tool especially suited for breaking straight cuts. The guide mark on the plier blade is positioned over the scored line, and the pliers are pressed slowly together until the glass breaks.

❱ *Circle Cutter*

If you cut out glass circles frequently, a circle cutter, which functions like a compass, is an absolute necessity. The suction cup at its center prevents it from shifting on the glass.

❱ *Glass*

The most important element in glass fusing is naturally the raw material—glass. Suitable types for this technique are opaque glass; transparent glass; stringers (also known as spaghetti glass or threads), which can be added as decorative elements; glass chips; and small glass shards (see page 11 for more information on glass). Of course, glass pieces to be fused together must be compatible (see page 26).

❱ *Ceramic, Ceramic Fiberboard, and Metal Molds*

Ceramic, ceramic fiberboard, and metal molds, available in various shapes, are used to help shape your glass into objects such as bowls or plates. See "Molds and Materials for Molds" on page 31 for instructions on using molds.

❱ *Ceramic Fiber Sheets*

Ceramic fiber sheets are available in thicknesses ranging up to 3/8" (1 to 10 mm) and are a suitable material for making unusual creations. (See "Molds and Materials for Molds" for more information.)

❱ *Pencil*

You should always have a pencil on hand for making spontaneous drawings of design ideas.

❱ *Metal Ruler*

A metal ruler suitable for working on glass has rubber strips on its back surface to prevent it from shifting on the glass. Used in conjunction with a glass cutter, this type of ruler is also an ideal tool for scoring straight lines.

❱ *Heat-Proof Gloves*

You will often need to open the hot kiln. These gloves will protect you when you do so.

Photo 2
The kiln used for fusing glass and for firing painted glass

18

❱ *Shelf Primer (or Shelf Wash)*

Molten glass sticks to every surface it contacts. To prevent this, you must brush or spray shelf primer (also known as "shelf wash" or "primer") onto any base or mold surface that the glass touches. Shelf primer is an easily-colored mixture of kaolin and alumina hydrate, combined in a ratio of 1:4. Directions for using it are provided in "Preparing and Equipping the Kiln" on page 25.

❱ *Glass Enamels*

Several projects in this book are not painted, but are sprinkled with Thompson glass enamels instead. You can draw patterns in these enamels after applying them. Enamels require an additional firing.

❱ *Stressometer (or Strain Viewer)*

The Stressometer (also known as a "polariscope" or "strain viewer") actually allows you to see the stress in fused glass. Directions for using this tool are provided in "Stress in Glass" on page 26.

❱ *Kiln*

Be sure to select a kiln that it is constructed for glass work. It must have heating elements both in its cover and on it sides, and you should be able to regulate these elements smoothly and independently of each other. With this type of kiln, you can make all the glass-fusing projects in this book as well as fire the painted projects in the second section. This kiln is also suitable for firing painted porcelain.

Safety, economy, and dependability are the essential features to look for when buying a kiln. Be sure the equipment meets all the safety requirements of your country. Various standard firing schedules are explained in "Firing and Temperature Schedules" on page 28.

❱ *Glass Grinder with a Cylindrical Bit*

A cylindrical-bit glass grinder is shown on page 24. You will need this piece of equipment to smooth the edges of cut glass.

Technical Principles

SCORING, BREAKING, AND GROZING GLASS

Because glass is a hard, brittle material, you need only score (or scratch) it in order to break it apart where you like. In addition to glass cutters, various tools for making scoring easier, including circle cutters and strip cutters, are now available.

Scoring Straight Lines

You can score a straight line by pulling a glass cutter alongside a ruler or by using a tool known as a strip cutter. To score glass with a cutter and ruler, first use a felt-tip pen to mark the scoring line on the glass. Then position the ruler with its edge about 1/8" (5 mm) from the marked line and apply a few drops of glass cutting oil at the beginning of the line. Next, hold your glass cutter against the edge of the ruler and draw it smoothly down the glass. If you do this correctly, you will hear a hissing or faint crackling sound as the cutter scores the glass.

A strip cutter must be attached to your work surface with screws, according to the instructions that come with it. Position the cutting head for the desired width of cut and apply several drops of glass cutting oil. Then use both hands to pull the cutter smoothly toward you.

In order to break the glass cleanly, hold it with both thumbs near the scored line, as shown in Photo 4. Break it apart slowly, pressing downward as you do.

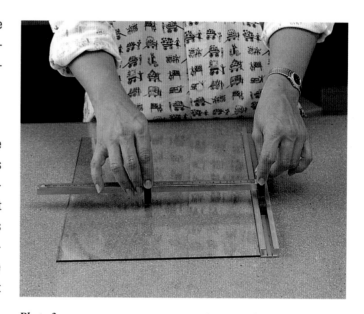

Photo 3
Scoring with a strip cutter

20

Photo 4
Breaking a straight cut

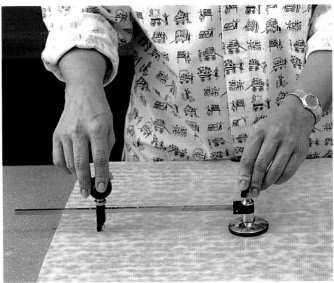

Photo 5
Scoring a circle

Scoring Circles

The simplest way to score a circle is to use a circle cutter. Set the desired radius on the cutter and position the suction cup on the glass so that when the cutter is rotated, its cutting head will remain on the glass. Then apply a few drops of cutting oil at the beginning of the scoring line. Press down lightly on the cutting head and guide it smoothly to score the glass. You should hear the hissing sound again.

Photo 6
Breaking a circle

Photo 6 shows the correct way to break a circle. First score the circle, as shown at the left. Then, using a glass cutter, score the four sides of the pane freehand and use your hands to break these pieces. Finally, use grozing pliers to break the four remaining pieces.

After breaking glass along a scored line, you'll often find that very small pieces of glass remain along the edges. These can be nibbled away with grozing piers. Position the pliers—curved side up—at the scored line and break off each small piece of glass by pressing toward the back (Photo 7).

Photo 7
Grozing

22 Freehand Scoring

To score freehand, first apply a little cutting oil to the beginning of the scoring line. Then place the glass cutter on the glass and push it along the line, in one continuous motion, to score the desired shape. When you do this correctly, you'll hear the slight hissing sound again.

Now take hold of the glass as shown in Photo 9. Hold your grozing pliers with the curved side up and use a gentle downward motion to break the glass close to the scored line. When there's sufficient glass on both sides of this line, you can also break freeform shapes by hand, as described in the section on scoring straight lines (Photo 4).

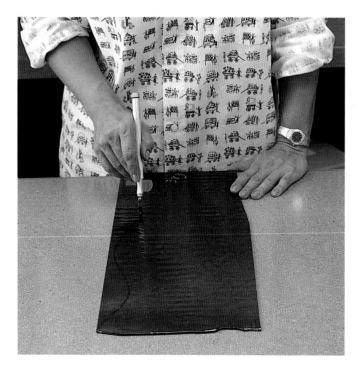

Photo 8
Freehand scoring

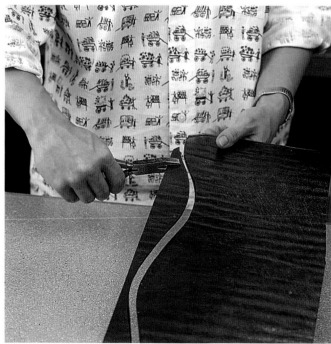

Photo 9
Breaking out glass with grozing pliers

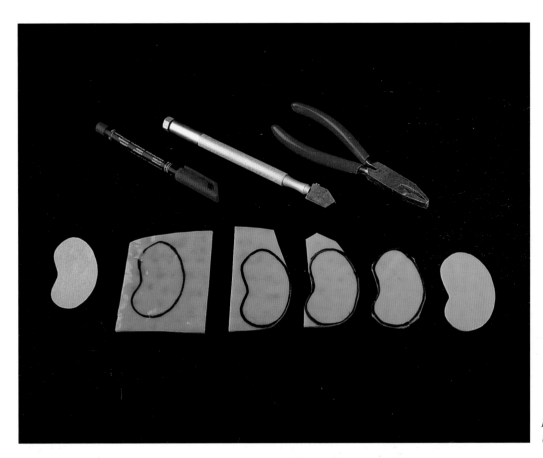

Photo 10
Using a pattern to score glass

Scoring with a Pattern

Photo 10 shows how to score glass by using a pattern. Place the pattern on the glass and draw around it with a felt-tip pen. Next, use your glass cutter to score along the marked line. Score auxiliary lines from the edges of the glass, to facilitate breaking the shape out. Then, using grozing pliers, break off the excess glass piece by piece. Finally, grind the glass shape as described in the following section.

GRINDING GLASS

24

In order to achieve an effective full-fuse firing, the edges of all glass pieces should be ground smooth. This is done with either a disc grinder or with a cylindrical-bit grinder. Straight or convex edges are best ground with a disc grinder. Concave edges, such as the one on the shape you scored using a pattern, can only be ground on a grinder with a cylindrical bit. When you set up your own workshop, buy the latter grinder first, as you can use it to grind any shape.

Photo 11
Grinding with a disc grinder

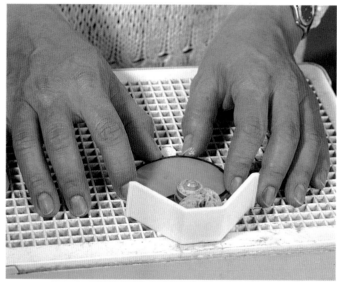

Photo 12
Grinding with a cylindrical-bit grinder

PREPARING AND EQUIPPING THE KILN

Paying careful attention to your kiln (see Photo 2 on page 17) and maintaining it well will pay off by yielding nicely fired pieces. The most essential part of every step of kiln work is cleanliness. Vacuum your kiln thoroughly before each step. Nothing is more annoying than finding small particles of insulation material fired onto a piece that would otherwise have been successful.

Photo 13
Spraying the kiln shelf

In addition to cleaning your kiln, you must coat or spray the kiln shelf (or a fiberboard or fiber sheet base if you use one), as well as any mold used for slumping or sagging, with shelf primer. This substance is available in powdered form from shops. For application with a brush, mix the powder with water in a ratio of 1:4. Then use a broad, soft brush to apply it to the kiln shelf, base, or mold, coating the surface once horizontally and once vertically. If you'd rather spray on the shelf primer, dilute the powder with water in a ratio of 1:6. I usually use an ordinary plant sprayer for this purpose. The danger of applying shelf primer with a brush is that undesirable traces of the brush will remain on the glass. This doesn't happen when the shelf primer is sprayed.

If you're using a mold with a smooth surface (a glazed ceramic or stainless steel mold, for example), first warm it to about 180°F to 210°F (80°C to 100°C) and then spray it while it is hot. The water in the shelf primer will turn to steam immediately, and the primer will adhere to the mold very well. If the mold is cold, the primer will run off its smooth surface. Each time you use a base or mold, clean off the burned-on shelf primer and spray the piece again as described above. Also, as was mentioned above, you must take great care to see that everything is meticulously clean when you prepare your kiln. All glass pieces must be washed thoroughly before you fire them. Fingerprints or other impurities leave ugly traces on both fused and slumped glass, so clean the glass well before each of these two firings.

STRESS IN GLASS

26 The unpleasant feature known as "stress" in glass is a red flag for many glass artists. Melting different types of glass together can cause various difficulties, but they're not as much of a problem when you understand your material. The chemical composition of glass is a major factor.

Most materials expand when heated and contract again when cooled. The same applies to glass. When two pieces of glass are fused together, their expansion and contraction rates must parallel each other; that is, the pieces must expand equally when warmed and contract equally when cooled. This movement in glass is referred to as the coefficient of expansion (or COE). Pieces of glass with the same coefficient of expansion are compatible and can be fused together. Attempting to fuse pieces of glass with different expansion coefficients is an invitation to stress during firing, which in turn will lead to glass breakage sooner or later. Unfortunately, you will experience glass breakage. Although the wasted efforts made during this learning process are always a shame, don't let them stop you from further work. As the saying goes, we learn from our mistakes.

It is possible to test glass for obvious stress. Cut a strip from one type of glass that you'd like to use and cut a smaller piece from another. Place the smaller piece on the larger one. Then fire this test strip by following the instructions for full-fuse firing on page 28. After the firing, check the test strip with a Stressometer (or strain viewer), which is a special lamp upon which the test strip is positioned. Look through the Stressometer lens, rotating it over the test strip as you do. If you see a halo around the smaller piece on the strip, then your glass is stressed and will sooner or later break when you work with larger pieces of it. Under extreme stress, the small piece of glass can even be torn off the test strip (stress tear).

The Bullseye company, in Portland, Oregon, manufactures tested, compatible glass that is very suitable for glass fusing. Bullseye carries a large selection of colors, so you won't need to set limits on your creations. This glass is guaranteed to be compatible and doesn't need to be tested. Of course, any two pieces of glass cut from the same sheet are always compatible, no matter which company has manufactured the sheet .

Photo 14
Top: Prepared test strip
Bottom: Fired test strip. The stress crack in the glass at the left is a result
of glass incompatibility.

FIRING AND TEMPERATURE SCHEDULES

28

A basic principle of glass fusing is that every piece of glass should first be heated very slowly to its strain release point. At temperatures above this point, the glass stops expanding. This slow heating is best executed using the heating elements at the top of the kiln. Cooling the glass down from the strain release point to room temperature must also take place very slowly. The firing process is very important and must always occur in five stages.

The Five Stages of Firing

❭ *1. Initial Heating Phase*

This stage, which should take anywhere from 90 to 120 minutes, is the one during which the glass pieces are heated from room temperature to their strain release point, which ranges from 930°F to 1000°F (500°C to 540°C).

❭ *2. Rapid Heating Phase*

The glass may then be brought to the desired fusing temperature very quickly (within 15 to 60 minutes, depending on the kiln you're using). Depending upon the size and thickness of the glass pieces, this temperature is sometimes maintained for 5 to 15 minutes, especially during a first, full-fuse firing.

❭ *3. Rapid Cooling Phase*

The kiln is now opened temporarily to cool it, but the temperature shouldn't fall below 930°F (500°C). Opening the kiln helps speed up the work. If you aren't pressed for time, you may also allow the closed kiln to return to the strain release point, or you may open the peepholes.

❭ *4. Annealing Soak Phase*

At the strain release point of 930°F to 1000°F (500°C to 540°C), the kiln temperature is maintained for 15 to 60 minutes, depending on the size of the piece of glass. This "soaking" time, during which the fused glass pieces are tempered by allowing their temperatures to equalize throughout, can never be too long. Always allow yourself sufficient time for this stage.

❭ *5. Cooling Down*

Before you open the tightly closed kiln, it must slowly return to room temperature.

To ensure satisfactory results, always follow these five steps exactly. Take note of them again.

– Slow increase of temperatures to the strain release point
– Quick rise to the desired fusing temperature
– Quick return to the strain release point
– Maintaining the temperature in an annealing soak phase
– Return to room temperature

In the upcoming projects, I will explain firing requirements as I have in the example below:

"Fire to 1490°F (810°C) and hold for 10 minutes"

Using the five-stage format, this means that a temperature of 1490°F (810°C) should be held for 10 minutes.

Note that I don't always mention the other firing stages in the project instructions. Read this section carefully and, for every firing you complete as you make the fused projects (full-fuse firing, slumping, sagging, and maturing of enamels), follow the firing steps described here—to the letter.

Average Temperature Ranges

Keep in mind that the ranges provided in this section are average ranges only and are suitable for fusing together two pieces of 1/8"-thick (3 mm) glass with or without small, decorative glass pieces on top. Actual temperatures will depend on your kiln, the size and thickness of the glass you are fusing, and the desired effects.

32° F to 1040° F (0° C to 560° C)

The phase during which all glass is heated to its strain release point; full maturing of all glass paints, lusters, and precious metal preparations.

1200° F to 1380° F (650° C to 750° C)

Slumping of glass in a mold. The steeper the sides of the mold, the higher the temperature must be.

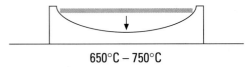

650°C – 750°C

Sagging takes place at lower temperature ranges because the actual weight of the glass aids the process even more than during slumping.

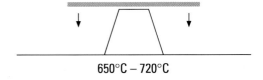

650°C – 720°C

1450° F to 1540° (790° C to 840° C)

Range of temperatures at which glass fuses completely (full fuse); the edges are completely closed and nicely rounded.

1600° F to 1710° F (870° C to 930° C)

At these temperatures, the glass begins to form bubbles and is very soft.

Please note: As mentioned earlier, these temperatures are approximations. You absolutely must get to know your own kiln by carrying out intensive test runs with it. Document every test run. The notes you keep will facilitate your creative work and will save you from unpleasant surprises.

An example of a test run for a full-fuse firing might occur as follows:

— Cut two pieces of glass, each 12" (30 cm) in diameter. Fire these, in five stages, to 1470°F (800°C).
    Result: The edges haven't melted or rounded off. The kiln wasn't hot enough.

— Run another test, firing two more pieces of the same glass to 1490°F (810°C).
    Result: The edges still aren't melted or rounded off. You must therefore run yet another test.

— In the next test run, heat the kiln to 1490°F (810°C) again and hold that temperature for 10 minutes.

— Run another test at 1510°F (820°C), and so on.

By advancing the temperatures until you're completely satisfied with the results, you'll discover the exact temperature for full-fuse firing of your selected glass in your own kiln. Proceed in the same way when slumping or sagging glass. Compare your results with the average temperature ranges.

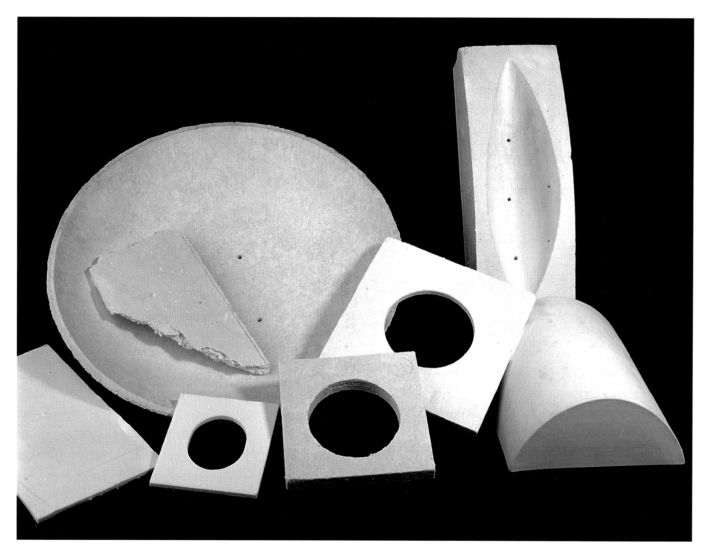

Photo 15
*Various materials for molds: Ceramic fiberboard,
ceramic fiber sheets, ceramic, and plaster*

MOLDS AND MATERIALS FOR MOLDS

Basically, any object that can withstand temperatures up to 1560°F (850°C) is suitable for use as a mold. Because soft glass sticks to all materials, however, you must always spray or brush shelf primer (or shelf wash) onto any surface that the heated glass will touch, including kiln shelves; ceramic and metal molds; and molds or bases made of ceramic fiberboard or fiber sheets. For flat firings (full-fuse firings), use kiln shelves made of cordierite (a type of ceramic material that doesn't move noticeably at higher temperatures) or ceramic fiberboard mats (a heat-resistant insulation material) as bases for the glass pieces.

❭ *Unglazed Ceramic Molds*

Unglazed ceramic molds are usually used as slump molds and as supports for sagging. You can also design and make your own from clay. If you model a clay mold yourself, make two to three little holes through its lowest portion so that during slumping, air won't be trapped between the glass and the bottom of the mold.

❭ *Ready-Made Ceramic and Porcelain Molds*

For slumping, ceramic and porcelain pieces can be used as molds. They need ventilation holes, however, which you must make yourself with a diamond drill. Because shelf primer doesn't adhere well to glazed surfaces, you must either heat the piece well and spray it while hot, or, before spraying the cold mold, roughen its glazed surface (use sandpaper or sandblast it). Not many people have sandblasting booths at home, but a metal workshop will certainly be able to do this job for you.

❭ *Plaster Molds*

Because you can cast them yourself, molds made from heat-resistant plaster are also very popular. The lifespan of this mold material is limited, however. You must also treat plaster molds with shelf primer before using them.

❭ *Ceramic Fiberboard Molds and Ceramic Fiber Sheets*

These materials can be worked very easily with a fret saw (for ceramic fiberboard) or with shears or a craft knife (for ceramic fiber sheets). Before you can use these materials with glass, however, you must fire them once to 1470°F (800°C) to burn out residual materials that remain from the manufacturing process. Be careful, as this firing will produce a lot of smoke and some terrible odors!

❭ *High-Grade Steel Molds*

High-grade stainless steel molds are best suited for sagging or for relatively shallow slumping. Most materials expand when warmed and contract when cooled. High-grade steel and glass do not move equally; the steel expands more than the glass during warming and therefore contracts more during cooling, so steel molds can damage glass that is slumped at steep angles. During sagging or shallow slumping, however, the piece can simply be lifted out of the mold.

Glass Fusing Projects

PROJECT 1 – PLATE

This plate, with small air bubbles that are characteristic of glass fusing, is decorative and useful at the same time. It will serve as the basis for the glass-painting project on page 101.

Cut out two glass circles, as described on page 20, and grind the edges smooth. After preparing the kiln and spraying the kiln shelf with shelf primer, place the two, carefully washed pieces on the shelf. Then complete a full-fuse firing, following the five steps on page 28, to a maximum temperature of 1490°F (810°C). Hold this temperature for 10 minutes.

To slump the glass, wash the fused discs, which should have nicely rounded edges and small air bubbles, and place them on a slump mold that has been sprayed with shelf primer. Fire the plate to 1450°F (790°C); in this step, the temperature is not held.

QUANTITY	MATERIALS	DIMENSIONS
2	Float glass circles	14-1/4" (36 cm) in diameter
1	Ceramic fiberboard slump mold	14-1/2" x 14-1/2" x 3/8" (37 x 37 x 1 cm) exterior, with 8"-diameter (20 cm) circle removed
	Shelf primer	

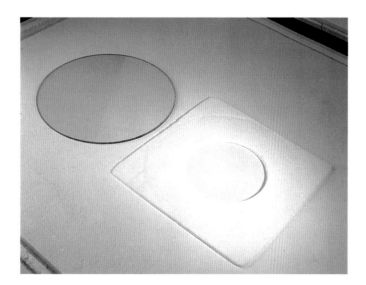

Photo 16
The circles of glass arranged for full-fuse firing; the slump mold

Photo 17
Plate

PROJECT 2 – FLAT WALL LAMP

34   The high degree of transparency of glass is a direct challenge when making a lamp. Glass lamps, whether painted or not, always give out a wonderful light. The wall lamp shown here, which we will also paint later (see page 104), demands some cutting skill.

First draw patterns for the lamp shapes on paper and cut them out. The cut pattern is shown in Photo 18. Then use the patterns to cut out the glass parts. Grind all parts after cutting.

Place the glass pieces in the prepared kiln. Photo 19 shows the correct arrangement. Do a full-fuse firing at 1510°F (820°C). Maintain this temperature for 15 minutes. Anneal/soak the glass for 15 minutes at its strain release point—970°F (520°C)—and slowly let the fused piece cool down to room temperature.

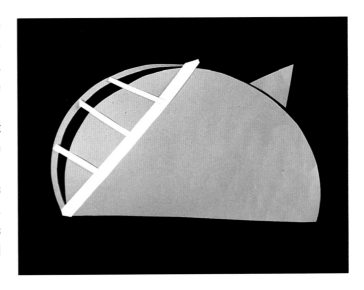

Photo 18
Cut patterns for wall lamp

QUANTITY	MATERIALS	DIMENSIONS
2	Float glass (brown pattern)	According to pattern
5	Float glass (white pattern)	According to pattern
	Shelf primer	

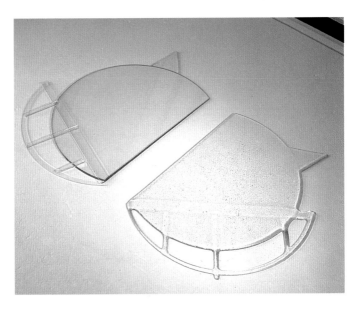

Photo 19
Arranged glass parts; the fused piece

Photo 20
Flat wall lamp

Photo 21
Blue soap dish

PROJECT 3 – BLUE SOAP DISH

QUANTITY	MATERIALS	DIMENSIONS
1	Cardboard pattern	About 6" x 4" (15 x 10 cm)
2	Bullseye glass (transparent blue)	According to pattern
1	Ceramic fiberboard mold, 3/4" (20 mm) thick	According to pattern
	Shelf primer	

This attractive soap dish lures you with its willful shape. In addition, it's the ideal size for cradling a piece of fragrant soap in an elegant way.

Make a pattern from cardboard in the desired, full-size shape. Transfer the pattern onto the piece of ceramic fiberboard and cut out the shape with a fret saw. Then draw the shape of the inner rim of the dish onto this fiberboard piece. To complete the slump mold, use the fret saw again to cut out the inner portion. Discard this inner piece. Fire the mold to 1470°F (800°C); then apply shelf primer to it. Don't forget to cover its cut edges as well. Use the cardboard pattern to cut your glass. Wash both pieces of glass thoroughly and execute a full-fuse firing to 1490°F (810°C). Hold the temperature for 10 minutes.

Next, slump the glass on the slump mold at 1440°F (780°C). The unusually shaped, transparent blue soap dish will lend a special accent to any bathroom. In the "Glass Painting" section of this book, we will embellish this dish with an elaborate platinum design (see page 96).

Photo 22
Fused glass pieces; slumped dish

PROJECT 4 – WINDOW DECORATION

On the one hand, a glass window decoration creates a privacy screen, and on the other hand, the light filters through it, and sunshine is refracted in a wonderful way. The play of light and shadow in the room changes with every ray of sunshine that enters. This is always appealing. The special charm of these window decorations lies in their shapes, which are modeled with pieces of ceramic fiber sheets.

In order to decorate the individual sections of this project by using ceramic fiber sheets, you must let your imagination reign freely. Punch or tear out pieces, braid strips, or cut out designs with a craft knife.

Photo 25 shows the exact sequence for producing one section. Arrange the fiber sheet elements in a decorative pattern and cover them with a pane of glass. Then lay a cross made from ceramic fiber sheet on top of the pane of glass. This cross will enable you to mount the individual elements together later. Lay a second pane of glass on top of the cross. Fire this section to 1510°F (820°C) and hold the temperature for 15 minutes. Finally, remove the fiber sheet material under running water, using a wooden stick to extract it from between the fused glass pieces. Photo 26 shows how many different possibilities there are for decorating individual glass sections.

QUANTITY	MATERIALS	DIMENSIONS
30	Float glass, 1/8" (3 mm) thick	6" x 6" (15 x 15 cm)
	Fiber paper sheets, ceramic fiberboard	
	Shelf primer	
	Copper rods and rubber rings for assembly	

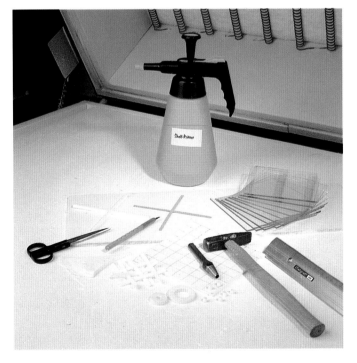

Photo 23
Required materials for the window decoration

Photo 24
Window decoration

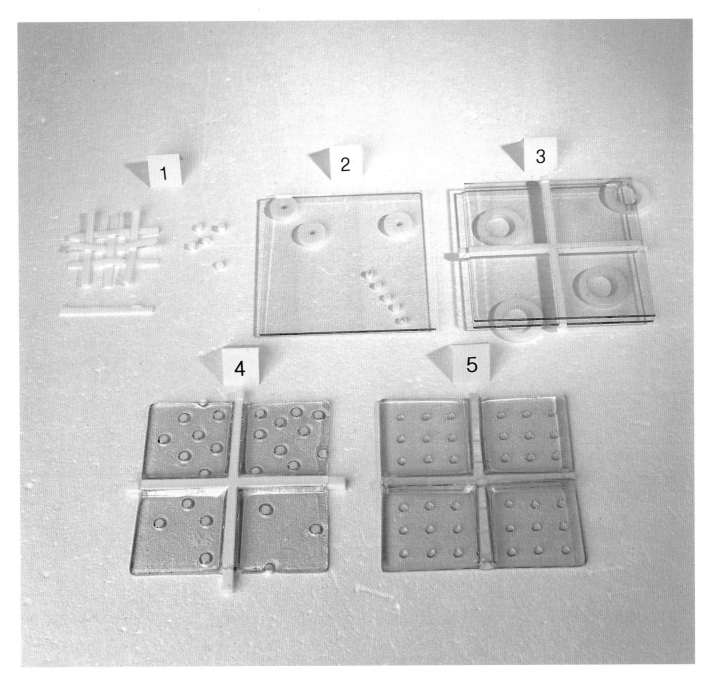

Photo 25
Stages of creating one section

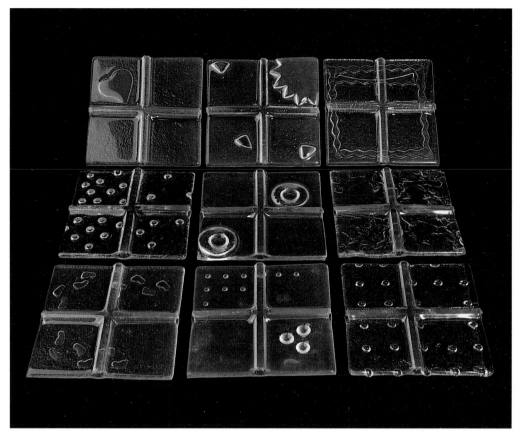

Photo 26
Decorative possibilities for individual sections

In order to assemble the individual fused sections, proceed as follows: Guide two fine copper rods through the crossed openings in one glass section. Before stringing other glass sections onto the copper wires, slip six rubber rings over each wire to prevent the glass sections from touching one another and getting damaged. These buffers also provide another special decorative effect. At the top of the window decoration assembly, bend the wires into a looped hanger. Along the sides and bottom of the assembly, bend the wires backward to rest next to the rubber rings, and trim each wire to 3/8" (10 mm) in length.

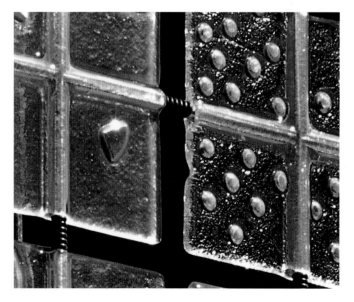

Photo 27
Detail of assembled sections

PROJECT 5 – JEWELRY

42

Jewelry you design yourself provides a lot of pleasure. A special piece of jewelry in a matching color on a favorite pullover adds the final touch to your outfit. In addition, making jewelry from glass is a good way to use up leftover pieces in a meaningful way.

Take several discarded pieces of glass (from your Bullseye glass, for example) and grind or cut each one to the desired shape. Then lay the parts in the kiln and decorate them with small pieces of glass or stringers (spaghetti glass or threads), and so on.

MATERIALS	DIMENSIONS
Leftover pieces of compatible glass	As desired
Bright gold Bright platinum	

Photo 28
Arrangement of glass for pieces of jewelry

Photo 29
Fused pieces of jewelry

Because the primary pieces are arranged in one layer and the second layer of glass is only decorative, we won't execute a classic full-fuse firing, but instead will fire to 1470°F (800°C), without holding the temperature.

I decorated several of the pieces with bright gold and bright platinum and fired them a second time to 1040°F (560°F). Instructions for applying these liquid precious metal preparations are provided in the "Glass Painting" section of this book (page 75). As a final step, you can use strong double-sided tape to mount ear clips or tie pins to the backs of the finished glass parts.

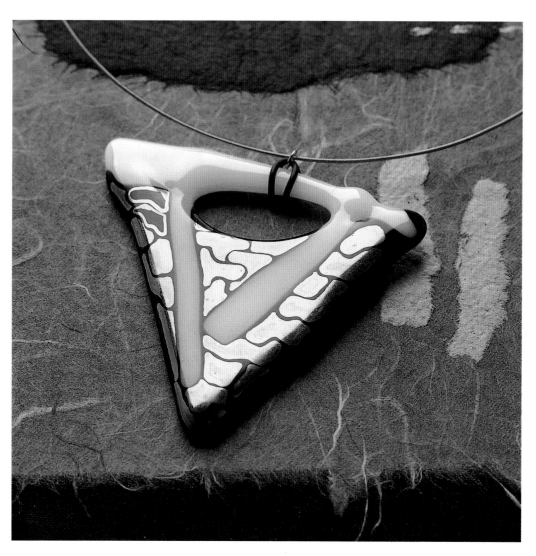

Photo 30
Jewelry

44

Photo 31
Jewelry

Photo 32
Jewelry

PROJECT 6 – NAPKIN HOLDER

Photo 33
Napkin holder

It would often be very convenient if paper napkins were at hand on the table or if notepaper were an arm's reach away from the telephone. This napkin holder helps keep order, serves as a decorative piece, and is a good place to start your work.

Cut the decorative glass pieces freehand from float glass, creating strips and round shapes as desired. Grind all the pieces carefully and wash them thoroughly. Sprinkle them with glass enamels in suitable colors and arrange them on the float glass. Place the float glass carefully on the sprayed kiln shelf. Then fire the pieces to 1470°F (800°C); because this project contains only one decorated layer of glass, you don't need to hold the temperature.

Place the decorated glass on the edge of an upright piece of 1"-thick (25 mm) ceramic fiberboard. Center the piece exactly and make sure that the glass is resting at right angles to the mold. The sag firing takes place at 1380°F (750°C) without holding the temperature.

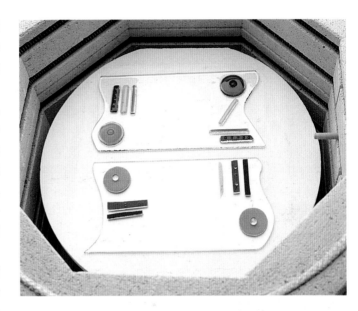
Photo 34
The napkin holder before and after firing

QUANTITY	MATERIALS	DIMENSIONS
1	Float glass	4-3/4" x 8-3/4" (12 x 22 cm)
As desired	Float glass circles and strips (for decoration)	
1	Ceramic fiberboard mold	5-1/2" x 5-1/2" x 1" (14 x 14 x 2.5 cm)
	Glass enamels (for decorative glass pieces)	

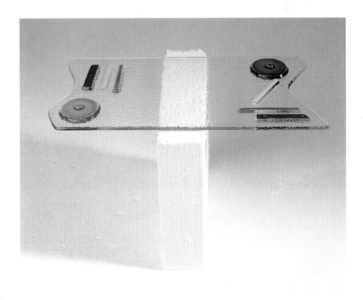
Photo 35
The piece positioned for sagging

PROJECT 7 – SMALL BOWL

48   Small bowls are always welcome for serving nuts or cookies or for holding all sorts of small items. When these bowls are made from recycled materials, so much the better. The technique of working with scrap glass ("junk de verre") is a welcome one when you have small remnants of compatible glass.

Wrap the scrap glass in an old cloth and sheets of newspaper. Using a heavy object or hammer, break up the little shards into fragments as small as you like. The smaller they are, the finer the specks of color will be on the final product. Wash the pieces of glass—a large sieve will be a big help— and allow them to dry well. Cut a supporting ceramic fiber- board mold, 3/8" (10 mm) thick. Then fill the opening in it with glass fragments. Complete a full-fuse firing at 1490°F (810°C) and hold the temperature for 15 minutes. Anneal/ soak the parts at 970°F (520°C) for 15 minutes. Then let the kiln cool slowly to room temperature.

Carefully grind the edges of the fused piece. Place a ring-shaped ceramic mold on three kiln posts and lay the sheet of fused glass on top. Because this sheet will be shaped in a free fall, its final form will be directly dependent on the firing temperature. The higher the temperature, the more the glass will slump. Photo 37 shows a bowl slumped at 1330°F (720°C). You can increase the temperature to 1380°F (750°C). Photo 38 shows two variations: the left-hand bowl was slumped at 1330°F (720°C) and the right-hand one at 1380°F (750°C).

Photo 36
Glass fragments arranged in the mold; the fused piece

Photo 37
The fused piece prepared for slumping; the bowl slumped at 1330°F (720°C)

Photo 38
Small bowls

PROJECT 8 – OVAL MIRROR

50

Mirrors are not only good for everyday use but can also serve as wall decorations. This oval mirror, with its colorful frame (also called a banner), can decorate any room in a special way. Choose colors to complement your furnishings.

QUANTITY	MATERIALS	DIMENSIONS
2	Float glass ovals	19-3/4" x 12" (50 x 30 cm)
	Glass enamels (transparent green, turquoise, and blue)	
	Stringers (or threads)	
1	Ceramic fiberboard mold	20-1/2" x 12-1/2" x 3/8" (52 x 32 x 1 cm), with centered, oval opening
	Shelf primer	
	Oval mirror	

Use a template to cut the oval pieces of float glass and the ceramic fiberboard mold. Grind and wash the glass pieces, following the instructions on page 24, and place them in the kiln for the full-fuse firing. Fire them to 1510°F (820°C) and hold the temperature for 15 minutes. For the second firing, place the fused oval glass plate on the fiberboard mold and slump it at 1470°F (800°C) without holding the temperature.

The frame is decorated with glass enamels. I used transparent enamels in green, turquoise, and blue, sprinkling them on through a tea strainer. Be careful to apply them evenly.

Photo 39
Fused glass on the slump mold; the slumped piece

Photo 40
Oval mirror

52

Photo 41
Applying glass enamel

Using a wooden stick, draw a pattern in the sprinkled enamel. Arrange stringers (or threads) in a contrasting color on the frame as desired. Place the piece and mold back into the kiln and fire on the enamel at 1440°F (780°C) to 1470°F (800°C).

Using the ceramic fiberboard mold as a pattern, cut out an oval mirror. Grind its edges very carefully and use very strong double-sided tape to attach it firmly into the slumped piece. In the same manner, attach a hook to the back of the mirror for hanging.

Photo 42
Enameled piece before and after firing

PROJECT 9 – ROUNDED WALL LAMP

This one-piece wall lamp illuminates the room in which it's placed in a mystical way. The play of its uneven surfaces is fascinating even when the lamp isn't lit and is serving only as a wall decoration.

QUANTITY	MATERIALS	DIMENSIONS
1	Bullseye glass (transparent)	10" x 12" (25 x 30 cm)
1	Bullseye glass (transparent blue)	10" x 12" (25 x 30 cm)
25	Bullseye glass (iridescent black)	3/8" square (1 x 1 cm)
As desired	Stringers (threads)	20-1/2" x 12-1/2" x 3/8" (52 x 32 x 1 cm), with centered, oval opening
	Ceramic slump mold	
	Shelf primer	

Take a fired, 1/8"-thick (3 mm) ceramic fiber sheet, sprinkle it with water, and press shapes into it with your fingers. Place this sheet, with its textured surface facing up, on the kiln shelf. Next, cut small squares and strips from iridescent black glass and arrange them on top of the ceramic fiber sheet, with their iridescent surfaces face down. On top of these, place one pane of transparent glass and one of blue glass. The full-fuse firing to 1490°F (810°C) follows. Hold this temperature for 10 minutes. Hold at the strain release point—970°F (520°C)—for 20 minutes and allow the kiln to cool slowly to room temperature. When you open the kiln, the piece will be lying on its lovely, decorated outer surface; you'll be looking at its back surface. Center the piece of glass exactly on the slump mold, positioning the decorative surface face up.

Photo 43
Decorative pieces arranged on ceramic fiber sheet and covered with clear glass; fused glass pieces viewed from the lovely, decorated outer surface

Photo 44
Rounded wall lamp

Now slump the lamp in a very slow firing. Raise the kiln temperature to 970°F (520°C) in 180 minutes, then very quickly raise it to 1200°F (650°C). Let the kiln cool to 970°F (520°C), and anneal/soak the wall lamp for 30 minutes. Finally, allow the kiln to cool slowly to room temperature.

Photo 45
The glass prepared for sagging

Photo 46
Sagged glass shape

PROJECT 10 – SQUARE BOWL

56

The iridescent and clear surfaces of this square bowl, complemented with fine gold decoration, are meant to remind you of the play of light on the surface of water.

QUANTITY	MATERIALS	DIMENSIONS
1	Bullseye glass (transparent)	9-3/4" x 9-3/4" (25 x 25 cm)
12	Bullseye glass (transparent grey)	2" x 2" (5 x 5 cm)
13	Bullseye glass (iridescent)	2" x 2" (5 x 5 cm)
	Square ceramic slump mold	
	Bright gold	

To make this shimmering bowl, first cut twenty-five small squares of glass and one large piece of transparent glass. Grind all the glass edges carefully, wash the pieces well, and arrange them on the kiln shelf (prepared with shelf primer) as shown in Photo 47. Make sure that all the squares lie flush with one another, with no spaces between them.

Now begin a full-fuse firing. Raise the temperature to 1490°F (810°C) and hold it there for 10 minutes. Allow the piece to anneal/soak for 15 minutes at 970°F (520°C). Then let the kiln cool slowly to room temperature. Use a pen to draw a fine design with the bright gold precious metal preparation (see the instructions on page 75); don't forget your signature. Then place the plate on the ceramic slump mold and fire it to 1200°F (650°C). This firing will simultaneously slump the piece and fire on the gold decoration.

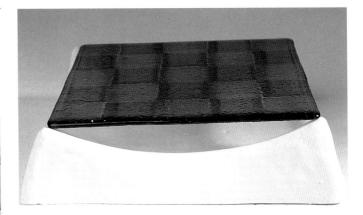

Photo 47
Arrangement of the glass pieces for fusing

Photo 48
Fused pieces for the square bowl

Photo 49
Placement of the fused glass on the slump mold

Photo 50
Square bowl

PROJECT 11 – ROUND BOWL

58

The reflections in a drop of water inspired me to make this bowl. Choose iridescent glass to evoke the shimmering of water.

To make this sophisticated round bowl, first draw and cut out the patterns, then cut a glass base from Bullseye opaque black. Use the paper patterns to cut the three other glass pieces and arrange them on top of the black glass base. I embellished the transition area from the iridescent piece to the clear glass with a transparent glass strip, and the border between the clear and milky glass with small, iridescent squares (see Photo 51).

Fire the plate first to 1490°F (810°C) and hold the temperature for 10 minutes. Anneal/soak the plate at 970°F (520°C) for 20 minutes. Then gradually cool the kiln to room temperature.

Remove the plate from the kiln and wash it thoroughly. Apply the glass decoration. To do this, it's best to position the fused plate in the kiln and lay the decorative elements directly on top of it. I first shaped the red stringer over a flame—a simple procedure. Use an ordinary candle; the flame of a multipurpose soldering torch is too hot. As soon as the glass is soft, you can bend it lightly by hand (see Photo 54).

QUANTITY	MATERIALS	DIMENSIONS
1	Bullseye glass (opaque black) for base	15" (38 cm) in diameter
1	Bullseye glass (iridescent black)	According to pattern
1	Bullseye glass (transparent)	According to pattern
1	Bullseye glass (white cat's paw)	According to pattern
	Stringers (or threads)	
	Bright gold	
	Bright platinum	
	Ceramic slump mold	

Photo 51
Arrangement of glass pieces for fusing

Photo 52
Round bowl

60

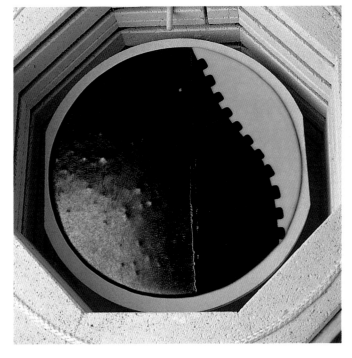

Photo 53
Fused bowl

The squares are covered with small pieces of yellow stringer (or thread). I placed small glass beads on the iridescent portion. Make these little beads beforehand as follows: Wrap a piece of transparent Bullseye glass in newspaper and smash it with a hammer. Then lay the small fragments in the kiln and fire them to a temperature of 1470°F to 1490°F (800°C and 810°C). Surface tension will cause the fragments to draw together into small beads.

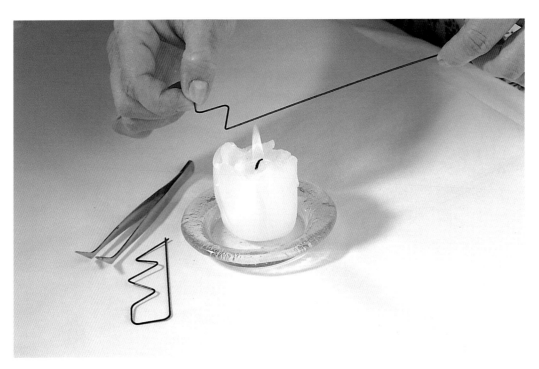

Photo 54
Shaping glass stringers (or threads) over a flame

Photo 55
The second firing at 1440°F (780°C)

Photo 56
Detail of bright gold and bright platinum decoration

Now fire the plate again with all its decorative elements in place. You don't want to melt the very small decorative pieces that cover the plate into the fused glass, so fire the plate to 1440°F (780°C), without holding the temperature.

Clean the plate again thoroughly and decorate it with bright gold and bright platinum (see the instructions on page 75). Then place the decorated plate on the ceramic slump mold and fire it to 1270°F (690°C), without holding the temperature. This firing guarantees an ideal slumping of the piece and at the same time yields lovely gold and platinum decoration.

PROJECT 12 – WALL ORNAMENT

The wall ornament is our most difficult fusing project, but the results are so special and ornamental that the effort required is certainly worthwhile.

If this type of object appeals to you, try to design your own shape, with colors that you've chosen yourself. I selected very strong, happy colors. Draw the wall ornament to size on a piece of paper, number all the parts (it's best to color in each section), and cut them out. Now they can serve as patterns for the colorful glass parts.

Cut all the parts from opaque white glass and then cut each one from colored, transparent glass, too. Play with the colors until you find a composition that pleases you.

Grind all the pieces and arrange them in the kiln, placing the opaque white glass pieces on the bottom and the colored ones on top of them. Place any desired decorations on the piece: glass stringers (or threads), Murini stars (pieces of patterned glass rods), glass beads, and small pieces of cut glass. Then do a full-fuse firing at 1490°F (810°C) for 10 minutes. Anneal/soak the piece for 20 minutes at 970°F (520°C) and let the kiln cool slowly to room temperature.

Clean the fused piece, set it back in the kiln, and add more decorative pieces to it. As well as the decorative materials already mentioned, add glass stringers (or threads) that you've shaped over a candle (page 60).

Fire the spirals once more, this time to 1440°F (780°C), without holding the temperature. This second decorating step will result in a structure similar to a relief.

One more step is required to complete the decoration. Clean the piece and apply bright gold and bright platinum. Don't forget your signature! The final firing is done at 1040°F (560°C), with top heat. Anneal/soak the piece for 20 minutes at 970°F (520°C).

Now you'll complete the wall ornament with glass elements, carefully cutting and cleaning them first, but you won't fire the piece again. Using patterns, cut the rays of red opaque glass (Photo 58). Grind these very carefully. Arrange the rays on the back of the spiral and attach them with strips of double-sided tape. Use the same very strong tape to fasten the hanger in place.

Photo 57
Wall ornament

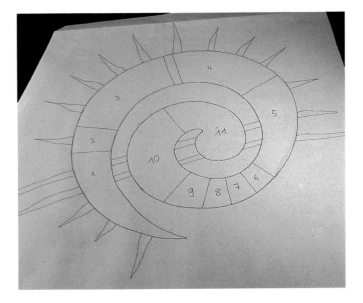

Photo 58
The pattern used for this project

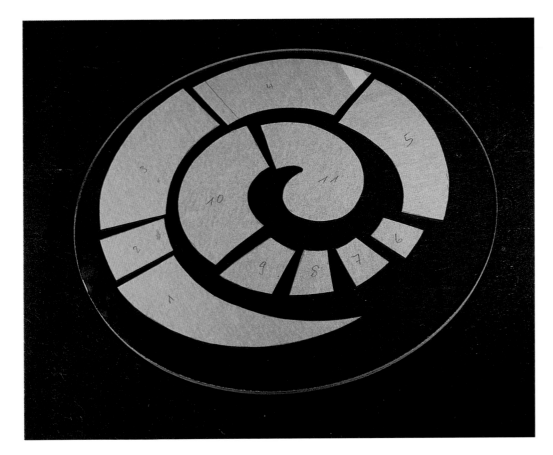

Photo 59
The pattern in use

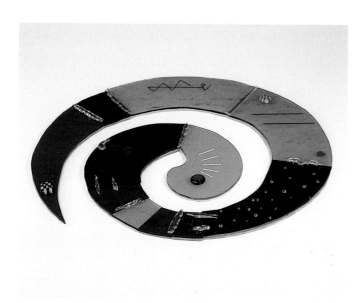

Photo 60
Arrangement of the pieces for full-fuse firing

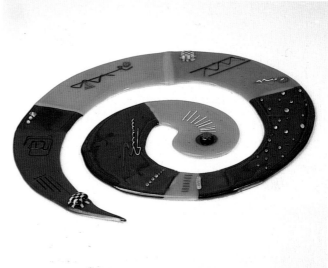

Photo 62
The spiral after a second firing at 1440° F (780° C)

Photo 61
The fused spiral

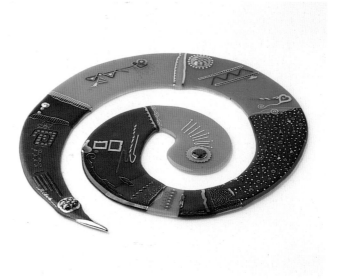

Photo 63
The finished, gilded spiral

Glass Painting

Important Information

In this section, I will pay special attention to glass painting and its unlimited design possibilities. Unfortunately, this fascinating and versatile technique is too little known, but with the work shown here, I hope to change this fact and spread my enthusiasm to many people.

Painting

Basically, any piece of glass can be painted. Most glass objects are made from soda-lime silica glass (see "What is Glass?" on page 11), which can be painted without any difficulty. Borosilicate glass, most frequently used in artistic objects made by glassblowers, is more difficult to paint because not all paints will stick to it. Painting crystal glass is also possible, but the glass itself is expensive. I've used various kinds of glass for the projects shown in this book; I often allowed an interesting form to dictate my choice. For your first attempts, select inexpensive glassware, which is very suitable for painting. Once you master painting techniques, you'll certainly want to try them on somewhat more expensive and unusual glass objects.

Correct Firing

The paints with which you'll be working must be fired in order to affix them permanently to the glass—a process that must be executed with great care. Buying a kiln with what's known as an "infinitely variable" temperature range will work to your advantage. The kiln must also have heating elements on its sides and top—elements that can be regulated independently of one another. (Kiln elements that don't function independently can be adapted by an electrician.) Firing glass paints requires sufficient air and direct radiant heat. Tall pieces, such as vases, are fired using only side heat. In contrast, flat pieces, such as plates, are fired with top heat only. Hollow glass balls such as Christmas ornaments are fired with 50% side heat and 50% top heat.

As with glass fusing, the following steps should be observed when firing painted glass: Heat the kiln slowly to the strain release point at 930°F (500°C), over a period of about 90 to 120 minutes; heat it quickly to the maturing temperature (1040°F or 560°C); lower the temperature to the strain release point and hold this temperature to complete the annealing soak phase. (This soaking phase is only necessary when firing painted pieces that include notably different glass thicknesses—a whiskey glass with a thick base, for example.) Allow the piece to cool to room temperature, with the kiln properly closed. Firing temperatures for each project are provided in the project instructions.

In glass painting, the quality of the glass to be painted plays an important role during firing. Soda-lime silica glass is fired at 1040°F (560°C). Borosilicate glass can withstand higher temperatures, up to 1110°F (600°C). Lead crystal glass, however, must be fired at a lower temperature—1000°F (540°C).

Equipment and Materials

68   When you're first starting out, you won't need every available paint, of course, and you can also do without the precious metal preparations such as bright gold and bright platinum. Build your palette of colors gradually. Over time, you'll want to experiment with applying bright gold and bright platinum.

   Additionally, you'll want to transform your glass work with some novelty, fantasy, and inspiration. After making several of the following projects, you'll know all the necessary basics and will be able to realize your own design concepts.

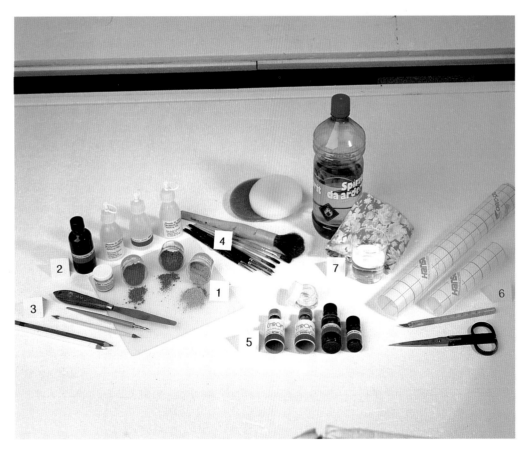

Photo 64

Required materials for glass painting. To be completely outfitted, you will need the materials listed below:

1. *A variety of powdered glass paints, including transparent and opaque, metallic, interference, and relief paints; crystal ice*
2. *Water-based painting medium and a compatible, water-soluble medium thinner; water-soluble outline medium; adhesive for the crystal ice*
3. *A white pencil for glass; pencil; wipe-out stick; pen; spatula; small, sandblasted pane of glass*
4. *An assortment of short- and long-bristled painting brushes; fine and coarse sponges*
5. *Bright gold and bright platinum; lusters; thinner for the precious metal preparations and lusters*
6. *High-quality clear adhesive film; scissors; craft knife*
7. *Water; lint-free cotton cloth; mineral spirits*

❱ Paints

For the glass painting projects in this book, you'll need both transparent and opaque paints. These are sold in powdered form and are mixed with water-based media before they're applied. Preparing powdered paint correctly is covered in "Mixing Paints" on page 70.

You'll also need a few other types of paint. White satin matte is a semitransparent white paint. Metallic and interference paints are paints with a metallic shimmer. Relief paints include white relief, black relief, and transparent relief. Transparent relief paint may be colored with opaque paint by mixing one part transparent relief with one part opaque paint.

❱ Painting Media

A water-based painting medium and a compatible, water-soluble thinner are necessary for mixing any paint that you intend to brush or stipple onto the glass. For creating fine-lined, pen-drawn outlines, you'll mix your paint with a compatible, water-based outline medium instead.

❱ Crystal Ice

Crystal ice is a form of ground glass that looks like salt before it's fired. It's used to create a rough surface on fired glass. A special adhesive is sold with the ice and is used to affix the ice to the glass before firing.

❱ Pens and Other Instruments

A pen is most useful for creating precise outlines with paint. You'll also need a pencil and a white crayon for making sketches and drawing on glass; a wipe-out stick (a wooden stick with a rubber tip) for applying relief paints; and a special spatula, which is used to mix paint with its medium by rubbing the two together on a glass palette (a pane of sandblasted glass).

❱ Brushes

It's wise to buy high-quality brushes because their strokes will be consistently better and softer. I use brushes with very soft bristles. Sponges are necessary in order to apply paints extensively and evenly when stippling.

❱ Bright Gold, Bright Platinum, and Lusters

Bright gold and bright platinum are precious metal preparations that round out any piece very nicely and lend it a subtle elegance. Lusters also provide wonderful accents when they're used correctly. You'll thin bright gold, bright platinum, and lusters with compatible thinners, ones which you can also use to eliminate small application mistakes from the painted glass.

❱ Clear Adhesive Film

Clear adhesive film serves as a resist by protecting glass areas that you don't want to paint. Use scissors or a craft knife to cut this material as desired.

❱ Water

Because the painting media you'll be using are water soluble, you'll need access to a water source in order to clean your utensils. Cotton rags and mineral spirits are also absolutely necessary for cleaning your tools.

Technical Principles

MIXING PAINTS

70

For excellent painting results, you must mix your paint and its medium very well. Unfortunately, this process (known as "pasting") isn't very popular because it's somewhat boring and requires patience when you'd rather start painting. For this reason, I suggest to my students that they use spatulas to paste their paints in advance, combining each paint with its water-based painting medium only. The paint may then be stored in a tightly sealed container, where it won't dry out. You can work with it for months, and its quality won't suffer at all when it's stored in this fashion. In fact, the mixed paint slowly expands a bit and becomes even finer.

To mix my paint, I use a very flexible spatula to rub the powdered paint and medium together on a glass palette. The medium with which the paint is mixed is odorless and is also water soluble, so you can clean all your utensils with water. I use an inexpensive, charcoal-free mineral water for this purpose, as very hard water can damage the paint and the tools over a period of time.

Begin the pasting process by placing about 1 teaspoon of the powdered paint onto the glass palette. Make a small depression in the middle, fill it with a compatible, water-soluble painting medium, and moisten all the powder. Then paste the paint and medium together thoroughly, pressing firmly on the spatula, until there are no longer any small lumps visible. The paint is the correct consistency when it falls from the spatula in heavy drops. You may return the paint to the jar at this point.

When you're ready to use the mixed paint, stir it briefly while it's still in its container, place the required amount on your glass palette, place two or three drops of a compatible, water-soluble medium thinner on the tip of your spatula, and mix it in until the paint is the desired consistency. The thinner makes the paint easier to apply by reducing its fat content and by making it more liquid.

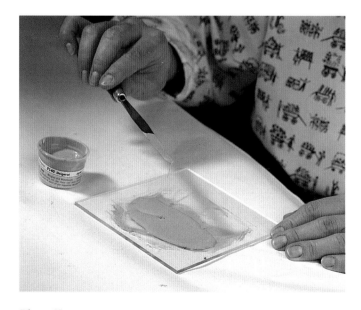

Photo 65
Mixed paint

STIPPLING GLASS WITH WHITE SATIN MATTE PAINT

White satin matte paint is commonly used in glass painting to make glass look as if it's been sandblasted; neither sandblasted glass nor glass treated with this paint is transparent. The matte surface serves mainly as a background for designs added in further steps.

White satin matte is applied with a soft sponge. In order to achieve very even results, I always use high-quality sponge balls. This paint can be difficult to mix. I paste it thoroughly on my glass palette and, if possible, allow it to soak for at least an hour or longer so that every last particle is mixed in, leaving me with a very fine paint. As with transparent and opaque paints, it's wise to paste the paint and medium in advance and return the mixed paint to its jar. The longer the mixed paint is left to soak, the easier it will be to apply.

When you're ready to start stippling, mix some of the paint with several drops of thinner on a glass palette. Then fold a small sponge twice and dab it into the thinned paint. If you pick up too much paint on your sponge, remove some of it by dabbing the sponge back onto the palette two or three times. Then begin to apply the paint to your glass, dabbing it on with quite a bit of pressure. To avoid unattractive sponge marks, be sure to use up-and-down motions as you do this.

After you've covered the entire piece with paint, use gentle stippling motions to distribute it evenly. To accomplish this, you may have to work over the glass piece two to three times. Aim for a thin, even application. Transparent and opaque paints may be stippled in the same fashion; applying white satin matte evenly is simply a more delicate task than stippling other colors.

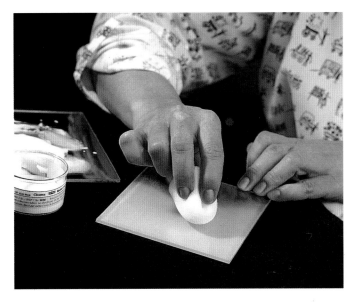

Photo 66
Motion used when stippling

Photo 67
Satin matte white roughly stippled, finely stippled, and fired

WORKING WITH A PEN

72

For creating outlines and the finest of details, the best results are obtained by using a pen. The paint, usually black, is first mixed to a liquid consistency with a compatible, water-based outline medium so that it can be applied effortlessly with the pen.

To make it easier to take up the paint with the pen, I always place the paint in a little dish, where it won't dry out as quickly as it would on a glass palette. If, after a time, the paint does get a little stiff, I add two or three drops of water and mix the paint again with a brush or stick. Add only water at this stage, not additional outline medium. You'll notice that paint mixed with outline medium dries more slowly than paint mixed with painting medium. You'll also notice that paints appear paler before firing than they do afterwards. Being able to judge what a paint will look like after firing takes some experience.

Photo 68
Working with a pen

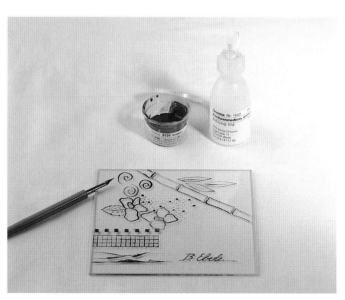

Photo 69
Completed, unfired pen work; required materials

WORKING WITH A BRUSH

Brush-painting techniques are similar to classical painting techniques. The shapes of flowers and animals are created by imitating the natural movements of the objects themselves. For smaller subjects, I use a high-quality, very soft brush with short bristles; for larger subjects, I use a long-bristled brush. The choice of brush is a matter of experience and of personal preference.

To paint a rose, as an example, mix separate batches of opaque beige-red and opaque dark red. Draw two opposing surfaces of the brush through the lighter color. Fill the brush with paint, but avoid overloading it. Next, draw one side of the saturated brush through the dark red paint. (If you draw the left side of the brush through the dark red, the dark red shading will appear on the left side of the rose you paint.) The more dark red you pick up, the darker the rose will be. The brush is now prepared. Place it on the glass, press it down, and guide it with a steady upward motion in a half-moon or C shape. Because this brush stroke serves as the basis for all smaller subjects executed in a natural manner, you must master making it to the left, to the right, and straight.

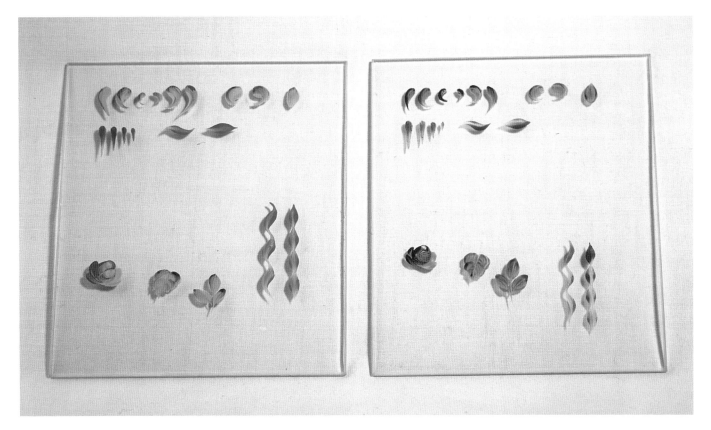

Photo 70
Unfired and fired pieces with basic brush strokes

Photo 71
Unfired and fired bright gold application, executed with a brush and pen

APPLYING PRECIOUS METAL PREPARATIONS WITH BRUSHES AND PENS

Bright gold and bright platinum are precious metal preparations that lend a glass object a final touch, a noble air, and a special effect. They're indispensable for glass painting. Ready-to-use bright gold and bright platinum, available from paint suppliers, consist of precious metals that have been enriched by the manufacturer with inert chemicals and thinner; their gold or platinum content ranges from 9% to 12%. Before firing, their colors are brown to black. After the inert chemicals in them burn off during firing, the results are wonderful gold or silver colors. Application of precious metals requires some skill because it's difficult to make any corrections once they've been applied; removing precious metals from glass is difficult. If even a trace of the metal remains on the glass, it will be visible after firing as a grey shimmer. It's also important to use separate brushes for bright gold and bright platinum applications. Precious metals are very prone to all kinds of contamination. The cost of these materials makes it wise to be very careful when using them.

For application, you'll need a soft, long-bristled brush. I prefer a good artificial bristle brush because precious metals are harsh on the bristles, and you'll need to replace the brush more often than you do for normal painting. The thinners for bright gold and bright platinum dry out the bristles, which tend to break off sooner. The thinners in many precious metal preparations evaporate quickly. If necessary, add two or three more drops of a compatible thinner and mix or shake the preparation well. Always make sure that you store your precious metal preparations in tightly sealed containers.

To apply bright gold or bright platinum with a pen, place a small amount of the precious metal preparation on a clean glass palette, add a little compatible thinner, and mix. Diluting the preparation with thinner makes it possible to apply very fine gold or platinum lines and other detailed designs, but be careful not to add too much thinner. Although precious metal preparations should flow easily from the pen, they shouldn't be too thin. I place my thinned bright gold or bright platinum in a glass container, where it's much easier to pick it up with a brush or pen. I store my precious metal brushes and pens in a small glass container filled with thinner and covered with a plastic lid into which I've punched two or three holes with an ice pick. I push the brushes and pens through the holes in the lid and let them hang submerged in the thinner, so that they're always ready to use and so that I don't waste any of the precious metal preparation. Thinners containing precious metals can be re-used.

APPLYING RELIEF PAINTS

76   Relief paints—as their name implies—leave a type of relief structure on the surface to which they're applied. Many relief colors are available. Among the most popular are black, transparent (which you can color), and white. All relief paints are mixed with compatible painting media to the consistency of toothpaste. Again, take note here: The paint must be thoroughly mixed with a spatula until it is very homogeneous. I use water rather than thinner to thin thickened relief paints.

   Relief paints are applied with a small tool known as a "wipe-out stick" rather than with a brush. First place some of the paint on the glass to be decorated. Then use the tip of the wipe-out stick to spread the thick paint, drawing the tool slowly over the glass as if you were icing a cake.

   Prior to firing, applied relief colors will seem pale and the lines will appear broad. During firing, however, these paints contract slightly and become a very effective type of decoration. Black relief is most often used for outlining flowers, animals, and so forth. For modern, more abstract painting, its use is unlimited. White relief also creates wonderful effects. The attraction of transparent relief is that it can be colored by mixing it in a ratio of 1:1 with opaque paint. This mixed relief is applied in the same manner as any other relief paint. One caution, however: Transparent relief paint shouldn't be mixed with other transparent paints. The resulting colors will always be grey.

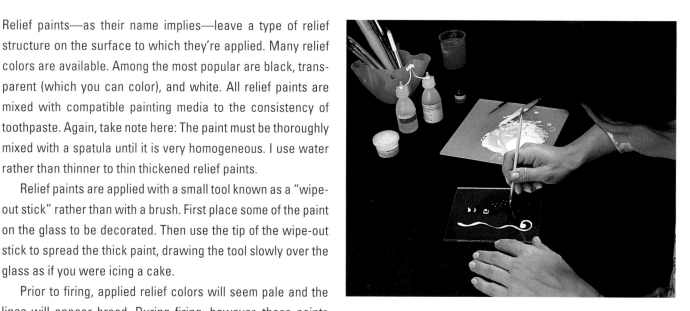

Photo 72
Applying relief paint with a wipe-out stick

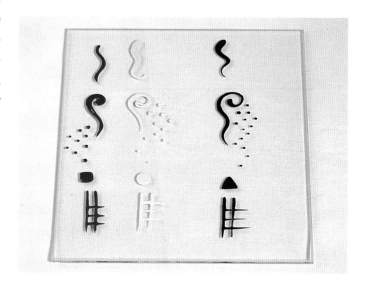

Photo 73
Fired applications of transparent relief, mixed in a ratio of 1:1 with dark blue; white relief; and black relief

APPLYING CRYSTAL ICE

Transparent crystal ice, which is most often used in modern painting, is white, and before it's fired, looks like salt or sugar. Its effect is a very special, irregularly raised surface. Working with this substance will seem a little strange at first, but don't let this stop you from experimenting with it; you'll soon be enthusiastic. Transparent crystal ice is available from paint suppliers in three grain sizes: coarse, medium, and fine.

In order to make it adhere to the glass prior to firing, you must use a special adhesive made for this purpose. Use a soft brush to apply the adhesive very thinly to the glass wherever you want the crystal-ice effect. Then pour the crystal ice over the adhesive-covered areas. Whatever sticks to the adhesive will be sufficient for a good effect. When I work with crystal ice, I always hold my glass over tissue paper, collect the excess ice, and return it to the container.

After firing, crystal ice is transparent. Of course, at this stage you may further enhance the surface with bright gold or bright platinum or with paint.

Photo 74
Applying crystal ice

Photo 75
Neatly applied crystal ice, ready for firing

Photo 76
Fired crystal ice in three grain sizes: fine, medium, and coarse

Photo 77
Fired interference paint on transparent glass and on a patterned black background

APPLYING INTERFERENCE PAINTS

Interference paints are reflecting paints, but in order to create the reflection effect, these paints should be applied to a dark background. A black background yields very good results; the paint has a wonderful effect on black glass. If you're working with a light glass, first apply a dark background paint with a brush or stipple a dark pattern; then fire the piece before applying the interference paint.

Interference paints react best when they're applied very thinly, so work according to the principle: "The less, the better." Mix the paint as usual, thin it with a few drops of compatible thinner, and add a few drops of water. Stipple this rather thin paint carefully and very evenly over the desired surface.

On transparent glass without any background paint, interference paint has a somewhat metallic effect, with a light color tone, and is a good alternative to the effect created with white satin matte. You'll be happy with the results.

Photo 78
Unfired and fired interference paint on black glass

APPLYING LUSTERS

Lusters are intensely bright precious metal preparations and are frequently used on porcelain. The gloss and shimmer of their surfaces have a very special charm on glass; lusters are a must for glass painting. They can be applied in a number of ways.

Applying Lusters with a Sponge

Dilute the liquid luster a little with a compatible luster thinner. Using a synthetic bristle brush, brush it onto the glass, and then dab it around with a sponge. Because the thinner evaporates quickly, you must work quickly. You'll probably want to discard the sponge as soon as you're finished, as it will be almost impossible to clean.

Applying Lusters by Floating Them onto Glass

Lusters may also be floated onto flat glass surfaces. Start by applying different colors of luster, drop by drop, onto different areas of the glass. Then use your gloved finger or a broad brush to mix each luster with double the number of drops of thinner. When you're finished, pick up the glass and gently shake it back and forth so that the lusters run together in a wonderful way. Dry the glass piece in an undisturbed place.

Applying Luster as a Film

Another method is to apply the luster as a film. Start by filling a glass or porcelain container with lukewarm water. Allow three to four drops of luster to glide from your spatula and onto the surface of the water (Photo 79), where the luster will form a film similar to the skin on hot milk. Wait a moment until the film has settled and no longer moves. Carefully dip the piece of glass that you want to decorate into the film and then rotate the glass slowly so that it will pull off all the luster.

The result is random but is always very effective. It's best to add further decoration to the piece by applying bright gold or bright platinum with a pen.

Applying Halo Lusters

A halo luster is a special type of luster that yields effects not possible with normal lusters. Use a soft brush to apply this luster over a large area and then use a long, pointed brush to draw the desired pattern—also with halo luster—onto the halo background. Very precise patterns can be executed in this fashion. The less luster you use for drawing, the finer the result will be.

Photo 79
Allowing the luster to glide onto the surface of the water

Photo 80
Taking up the luster film

Photo 81
Applying halo luster

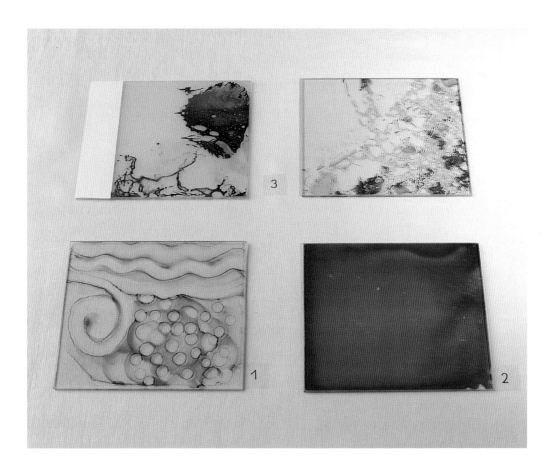

Photo 82
Fired lusters:
1. Halo luster
2. Sponged luster
3. Two examples of floated luster

82

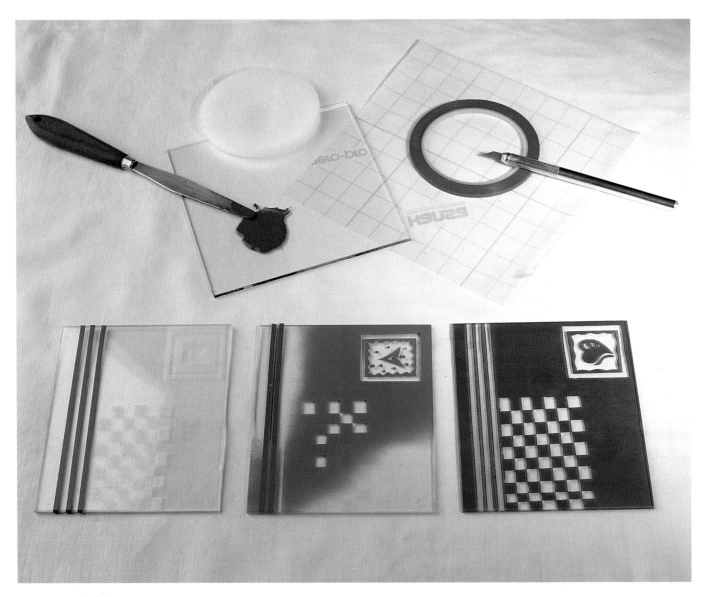

Photo 83
Working with clear adhesive film
Applied film (left); stippled piece (center); fired piece (right)

WORKING WITH CLEAR ADHESIVE FILM

In order to apply paints very precisely when I'm creating a defined pattern, I always work with a clear adhesive film that sticks slightly to the glass. This resist technique is especially good for creating geometrical and very small designs, and straight lines become child's play. You'll have to get used to using this film, but once you do, you won't be able to—or want to—do without it. Its advantages become evident the longer you work with it.

As usual, I wash the glass very carefully. Then I stick an original design pattern onto its back surface. If possible, I cover the entire piece of glass with clear adhesive film. To keep the film from creasing when you're covering contoured areas, you'll need to cut out wedge-shaped openings so that the film can be pressed firmly onto the glass. Next, I use a pencil to trace my design pattern onto the adhesive film and then I cut out sections of the film with a craft knife. Once you've practiced using a craft knife long enough, the traced pattern becomes superfluous; you'll be able to cut the design freehand. After I've cut the design from the adhesive film, I stipple the entire surface with well-mixed paint.

Photo 84
Cutting the film

Photo 85
Stippling paint over the film and glass

84 Then I let the paint dry. If I'm in a hurry, I dry the paint by heating the glass in a kiln at 176°F (80°C) for 15 minutes. Under no circumstances should you dry the painted piece in a kitchen oven; even at this low temperature, if the paint contains lead particles, they will be released and can settle on the oven's heating elements. These particles, which are dangerous to your health, can contaminate food. When the paint is dry, I use the tip of my craft knife to remove the remaining clear adhesive film before firing.

Photo 86
Removing the remaining film

WORKING WITH A LIQUID RESIST

It's almost impossible to recreate freehand-drawn shapes with clear adhesive film. A different technique is best suited for this job—working with a liquid resist. I've found that the decal covercoat normally used with decal printing on glass is very suitable for this purpose, but it must be applied very thickly and must be thoroughly dry before paint or luster is applied over it. The dried film that it forms, which can be pierced with a pointed instrument and then peeled off, is resistant both to water (and therefore to paints mixed with water-based painting media) and to the thinners used with lusters, bright gold, and bright platinum.

Photo 87
Working with liquid resist
Applied resist; painted glass with resist removed; fired, finished piece

DECAL PRINTING

Decal printing makes it possible to achieve effects that are otherwise impossible or very difficult to achieve directly on glass. The painting techniques that are possible with decals include stamping, printing, finger painting, applying paint with a roller, spattering paint with a toothbrush or sieve, creating painted paper cutouts, and engraving—and these are only a few suggestions as to how decal printing can be used.

Working with decals involves three basic steps. First, you apply paint onto a special transfer paper known as "decal paper." Then you cover the paint with a liquid substance called a "decal covercoat." Finally, you transfer the paint and covercoat to the glass piece.

For decal work, mix your powdered paint with a decal medium for silk screening, in a ratio of 1:1. Then, using a brush with thick bristles, a synthetic roller, or your gloved fingers, apply the paint to the shiny side of a sheet of decal paper. You may want to try other techniques, such as rolling out a thin coat of the paint onto your glass palette and transferring it onto decal paper that has the stamp of your firm on it. This is a simple way to produce glassware with your firm's name on it. Children use potato stamps in a similar fashion. Another technique is to apply the paint to the decal paper and then use a wooden stick or kitchen spatula to draw a pattern in it. You can also apply the paint to only one half of the sheet, fold the sheet closed, press it together tightly and unfold it again. (You can create very effective butterflies in this manner.) Give free reign to your imagination.

Allow the paint to dry thoroughly on the decal paper. This takes approximately one day. Then use a synthetic roller to cover the painted areas of the sheet with a decal covercoat. Be sure to apply the covercoat in an even layer and allow it to dry completely for about one day.

The result will be a decal that you've produced yourself, one which you may use whole or cut into individual pieces to make, for example, paper cutouts. To transfer the decal (the paint and covercoat) onto the glass, first fill a basin—one large enough to hold the decal paper—with lukewarm water. Submerge the decal paper in the water, using your hands to hold it flat so that it won't roll up. After a short time, the covercoat and paint will separate from the decal paper. Position this covercoat/paint film on the piece of glass and dab it with a soft cloth until it is flat. Be careful that no bubbles remain under the film. Use a needle to pierce any that you see and press any water out. After firing, bubbles leave ugly traces that are difficult to disguise or correct. If the film has been applied correctly, the piece can be fired to 1040°F (560°C).

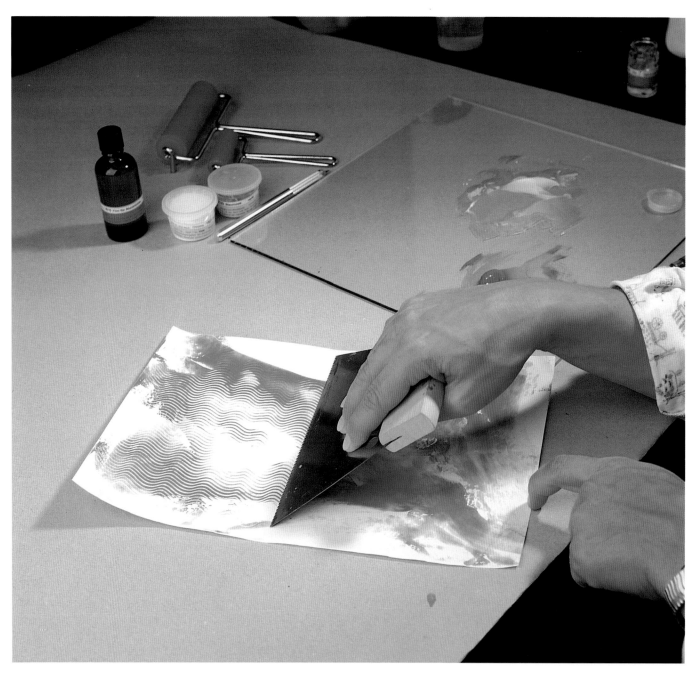

Photo 88
Applying paint to decal paper

Photo 89
Rolling decal covercoat over the dried paint

Photo 91
Separating the film from the decal paper

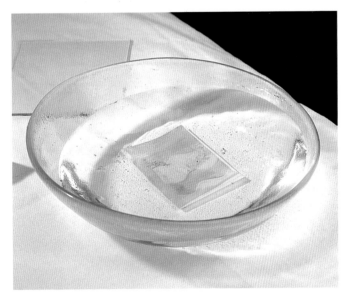

Photo 90
Soaking the decal

Photo 92
Pressing the decal onto the glass

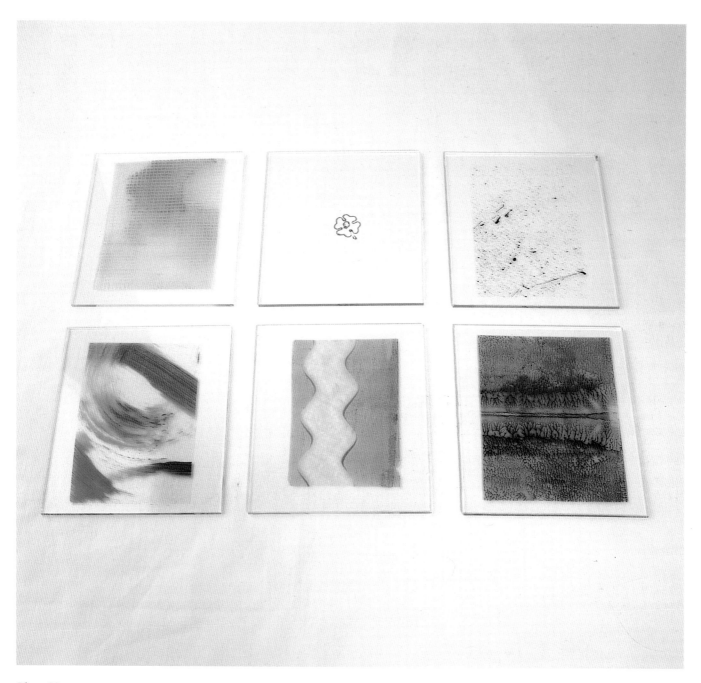

Photo 93
Fired decals produced in a variety of ways

90

Photo 94
Applying dry paint with a large brush

APPLYING DRY PAINT

Rather than mixing your paint by rubbing liquid into it, you may apply dry powdered paint directly to glass. For dry application, you'll need paint, a very thick, soft brush, and the same adhesive that is used with crystal ice. A broad, rounded cosmetics brush is best suited for this job.

Either brush or stipple a thin coat of the crystal-ice adhesive onto the desired areas of the glass. Then empty the powdered paint onto a glass palette and take it up with the cosmetics brush. (You may also work directly from the paint container.) Dab the brush very gently onto the adhesive-coated areas of the glass. Be careful not to contaminate your brush with the adhesive, or a nice color application won't be possible.

Photo 95
Unfired and fired dry paint applications

Glass Painting Projects

PROJECT 1 – GLASS ORNAMENTS

92

This decorative ball doesn't necessarily have to disappear into the drawer after the holidays. It can provide pleasure year round by beautifying either a window or a dark corner.

MATERIALS	COLORS
Decorative glass balls	
Satin matte paint	White
Interference paint	Violet red
Interference paint	Steel blue
Luster	Yellow
Luster	Carmine
Luster	Blue
Bright gold	
Liquid resist (decal covercoat)	
Painting medium	
Painting medium thinner	
Luster thinner	
Fine sponge	

Apply thick liquid resist, in small patterns, onto the balls. Allow these patterns to dry thoroughly, then stipple one ball with white satin matte, one with violet red interference, and one with steel blue interference. Allow the paints to dry well, remove the dried resist film with a pointed object such as a craft knife, and fire the balls to 1040°F (560°C), using 50% side heat and 50% top heat.

As a second step, refine the decoration. Gild the balls first. With a brush, add luster accents in shades of yellow, carmine, and blue. Finally, sign the balls and fire them to 1040°F (560°C) again, using 50% side heat and 50% top heat. You don't have to soak these ornaments at the strain release point.

Photo 96
Glass ornament

Photo 97
Glass ornament

94

Photo 98
Glass ornament primed with violet red interference

Photo 99
Glass ornament primed with satin matte white

Photo 100
Glass ornament primed with steel blue interference

PROJECT 2 – CANDLE HOLDER

This holder was made from a commercial black glass plate. The metallic shimmer of its black surface lends it a mystical appearance. Depending on the designs you select, you can create a very personal gift in a relatively quick and uncomplicated manner.

Cover the border of the black plate generously with clear adhesive film, cut your design, and stipple the plate very lightly with violet red and steel blue interference paints. Peel off the film only after the paint is completely dry. Using top heat, fire the glass to 1040°F (560°C). Sign the holder on the bottom.

Photo 101
Candle holder

MATERIALS	COLORS
Black glass plate	
Interference paint	Violet red
Interference paint	Steel blue
Painting medium	
Painting medium thinner	
Clear adhesive film	
Fine sponge	

PROJECT 3 —BLUE SOAP DISH

96

This fused soap dish is one of the projects from the first section of this book. Even without additional decoration, the blue glass is highly ornamental, but with generous bright platinum decoration, the project will add a special touch to your guest bathroom.

Instructions for making the dish are on page 37. Use a brush and pen to add the bright platinum design. Because it's extremely difficult to correct mistakes made with bright platinum, carefully plan your design from the start. Check and sign the piece. Then, using top heat, fire it to 1040°F (560°C).

MATERIALS
Blue soap dish from page 36
Bright platinum

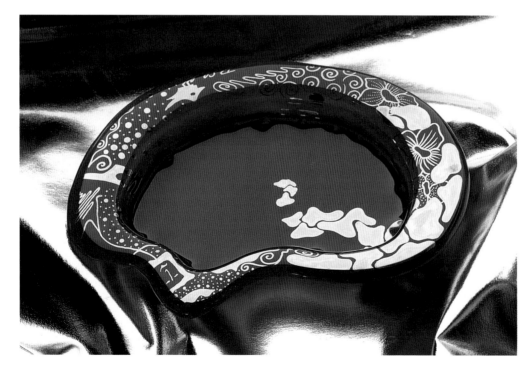

Photo 102
Blue soap dish with bright platinum decoration

PROJECT 4 – LANTERN

Photo 103
Lantern

I chose a simple whiskey glass for this lantern. When the candle glows through the crystal ice, it spreads a wonderful light. I was inspired by water splashing over a stone and for that reason, I chose to combine crystal ice with the colors shown here.

98

MATERIALS	COLORS
Whiskey glass	
Opaque paint	Black
Opaque paint	Dark red
Interference paint	Steel blue
Bright platinum	
Crystal ice, coarse	
Adhesive for crystal ice	

Apply the crystal-ice adhesive in various designs onto the whiskey glass. Sprinkle these areas with coarse crystal ice. When the adhesive is dry, check the glass to make sure the crystal ice has been applied only where desired. Using side heat, fire the glass to 1040°F (560°C). Because the glass has a thick base, during this firing—and the next two firings—you must anneal/soak it at 970°F (520°C) for 15 minutes.

Apply a thin coat of crystal-ice adhesive over the entire glass, except where the crystal ice has already been applied, and apply dry opaque black, opaque dark red, and steel blue interference (see page 91). Fire the glass a second time to 1040°F (560°C), also using side heat.

Next, apply bright platinum to several areas, add red accents, and sign the piece. Fire once more to 1040°F (560°C).

Photo 104
Applied crystal ice

Photo 105
Fired application of dry paint

PROJECT 5 – HANGING LAMP SHADE

Photo 106
Lamp shade

100

Photo 107
White satin matte application

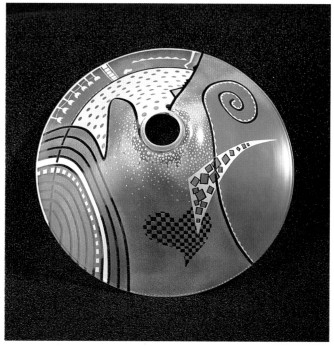

Photo 108
Metallic silver application

My goal when making this project was to create a lovely, neutral lamp shade that would fit into many different surroundings. With its various white designs, the shade spreads a wonderful, soft, unobtrusive light.

Cover the shade carefully with clear adhesive film, cut out your design, and stipple on a thin and very even coat of white satin matte. Remove the film. Fire the shade for the first time to 1040°F (560°C), using top heat.

Cover the lamp shade with clear adhesive film again, cut out a design, and stipple on the silver metallic. Remove the film and, using top heat, fire the shade to 1040°F (560°C) again.

Apply the additional design elements in white relief and bright gold. Then add the accents. Sign the piece and fire it a final time, again using top heat, to 1040°F (560°C).

MATERIALS	COLORS
Glass lamp shade	
Satin matte paint	White
Metallic paint	Silver
Relief paint	White
Bright gold	
Painting medium	
Painting medium thinner	
Fine sponge	
Clear adhesive film	

PROJECT 6 – PLATE

Photo 109
Plate

I've found that the simple shape of a flower bud goes well with the simple shape of this plate, which we made in the fused-project section (page 32). The contrast of the geometric designs and the soft shapes on the plate lend it a special effect. This project is truly a joy to use.

Make a drawing of your desired design. Stick this onto the underside of the plate. Cover the rim of the plate with clear adhesive film. Trace the drawing onto the film, and then remove the paper drawing. Using a craft knife, carefully cut the patterns from the clear adhesive film. This is best done against a light background so that the traced pencil lines are easy to see. Remove the sections of film that cover the surfaces you plan to stipple. Stipple these areas very carefully with white satin matte. When the paint is completely dry, remove the adhesive film from the bamboo and apply bright gold to the entire bamboo stalk. Remove the rest of the film and fire the plate, using top heat, to 1040°F (560°C). Anneal/soak for 15 minutes at 970°F (520°C).

Now use a brush to paint the flower with opaque dark red. Create its background with a thin coat of paint, diluted with painting medium thinner. Use a normally diluted coat of paint to shade the flower. With a clean brush, outline the flower. Apply the background and shading to the leaf and stem in the same manner, using transparent green and opaque black. Using a pen and opaque black paint mixed with outline medium, draw the outlines of the bamboo stalk. Fire the plate a second time, using top heat, to 1040°F (560°C) and anneal/soak again for 15 minutes at 970°F (520°C).

Shade the bamboo with opaque black. Intensify the shading of the flower by using dark red; for the leaves and the stalk, use opaque black. Dip the tip of a wipe-out stick into the opaque dark red and add red dots to the flower. Sign the piece. Complete the last firing at 1040°F (560°C), using top heat. Once again, anneal/soak for 15 minutes at 970°F (520°C).

102

MATERIALS	COLORS
Plate from page 32	
Satin matte paint	White
Opaque paint	Dark red
Transparent paint	Green
Opaque paint	Black
Bright gold	
Painting medium	
Painting medium thinner	
Outline medium	
Clear adhesive film	
Fine sponge	

Photo 110
Plate with white satin matte and bright gold

Photo 111
Painted plate after the second firing

PROJECT 7 – FLAT WALL LAMP

104

This fused wall lamp was also one of projects in the first section of this book. Because its shape is so pleasing, you could use it as a lamp without painting it, but the light shining through it will be much more interesting if you decorate the surface as well. The painted lamp will also be more noticeable when it isn't lit.

Cover the arch and beam with strips of clear adhesive film and cut the film as shown in the photo. Use a thick brush and circular motions to paint and shade the crowns of the trees. The best way to do this is to work with two colors at once, that is, with one color on one side of the brush and the other on the other side. Ideally, applying paint in this manner can be simplified by using a turntable as you hold the brush steadily with one hand. Next, stipple the arch and beam with opaque black paint. Fire the lamp to 1040°F (560°C), using top heat.

MATERIALS	COLORS
Wall lamp from page 34	
Metallic paint	Silver
Satin matte paint	White
Opaque paint	Black
Opaque paint	Dark red
Opaque paint	Dark blue
Opaque paint	Blue-black
Transparent paint	Dark blue
Transparent paint	Blue-green
Transparent paint	Ruby
Transparent paint	Topaz
Bright platinum	
Painting medium	
Painting medium thinner	
Outline medium	
Fine sponge	
Clear adhesive film	

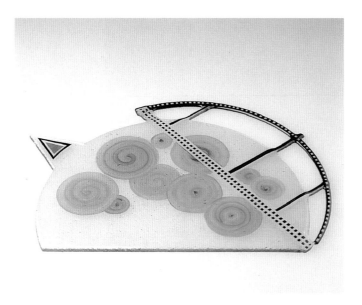

Photo 112
Primed wall lamp

Photo 113
Wall lamp

106   For the second step, cover the entire lamp with clear adhesive film and draw the outlines of the background with a waterproof felt-tip pen. Cut out these background designs carefully with a craft knife. Remove the film from the parts to be stippled and stipple with silver metallic paint. When the paint is completely dry, draw in the trunks of the trees with a pen and black paint. Give each tree trunk an individual pattern. Remove all the film and check the lamp for irregularities. Fire the piece for a second time at 1040°F (560°C), using top heat.

Shade the tree crowns with colors darker than their backgrounds. Finish the bow and the beam with bright platinum and sign the piece. When the paints and bright platinum are completely dry, turn the lamp over and stipple its back surface very lightly with white satin matte. Place the lamp in the kiln, propping it up with tiny pieces of ceramic fiber sheet to protect the stippled back surface. The paper will leave faint marks, so place it under sections that haven't been painted with transparent paint. The final firing is at 1040°F (560°C), with top heat. Anneal/soak at 970°F (520°C) for 15 minutes.

Photo 114
Wall lamp with background and trees

PROJECT 8 – VASE

This vase, with its headstrong form, demands unusual decoration. I chose a geometric pattern with a playful background. The vase looks very nice with a white flower and a leaf in it, but is also very attractive when empty.

Cut 1" (2.5 x 2.5 cm) squares of clear adhesive film and distribute them evenly over the vase. Then use a craft knife to cut out patterns from them. Be careful to execute this step precisely. Next, apply 1/4" x 1/4" (5 x 5 mm) squares of adhesive film over the rest of the background. Check your work carefully and make sure you've removed the film from all your cut designs. Use a cloth and mineral spirits to clean off any noticeable fingerprints on the glass. Now stipple white satin matte over the entire vase. When the paint has dried, remove all the adhesive film and check the vase for irregularities or mistakes. If you find any, scrape them off with a craft knife. Remove the paint dust with a large, soft brush such as a cosmetic brush.

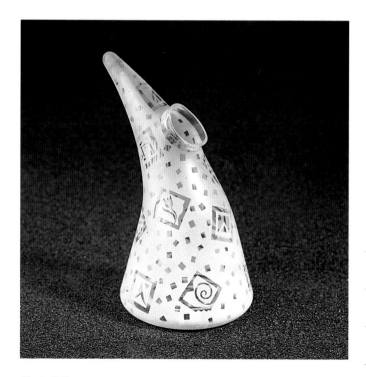

Photo 115
Vase stippled with white satin matte

MATERIALS	COLORS
Glass vase	
Satin matte paint	White
Transparent paint	Yellow
Transparent paint	Green
Transparent paint	Blue
Transparent paint	Purple
Transparent paint	Ruby red
Relief paint	White
Bright gold	
Painting medium	
Painting medium thinner	
Fine sponge	
Clear adhesive film	

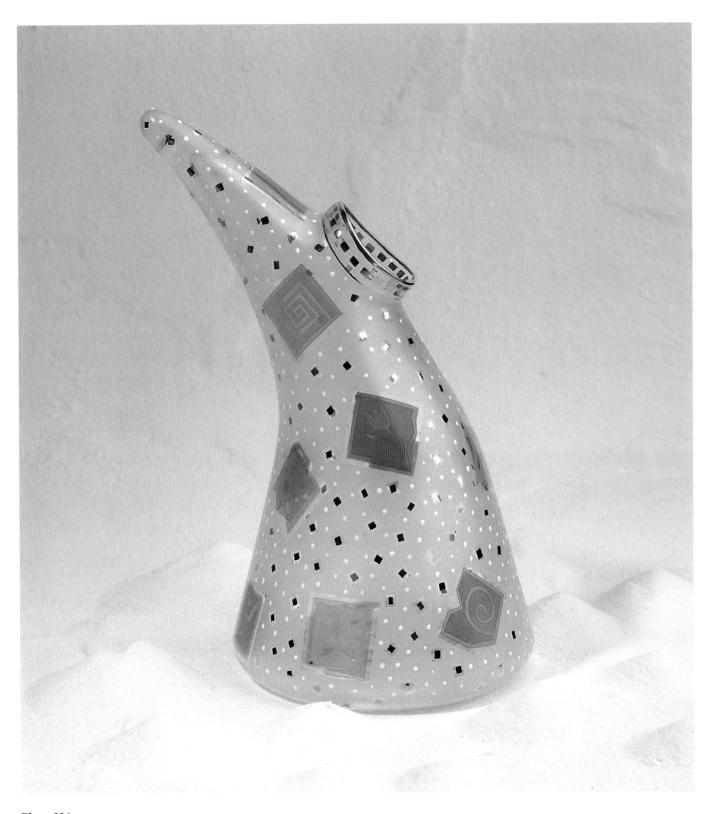

Photo 116
Vase

Fire the vase in the following manner: Using side heat, fire to 1040°F (560°C) over a period of 150 minutes and hold at this temperature for 10 minutes. Then anneal/soak at 970°F (520°C) for 20 minutes. Allow the kiln to reach room temperature, as always, with the lid closed.

Cover the edges of the large squares with strips of film in order to protect the white satin matte background. Then stipple the squares alternately, using the transparent paints listed above. Allow the paints to dry well before you remove the film. You may also dry the paints by placing the piece in the kiln for 15 minutes at 140°F (60°C). Check the vase again for irregularities and mistakes. The second firing also takes place at 1040°F (560°C), but this time the temperature isn't held.

Now embellish the background. Use a pen to add bright gold to the squares (see page 75). Apply dots of white relief over the rest of the background (application instructions are on page 76) and a little bright gold to the upper edge of the vase opening. Now only your signature is missing. The third firing takes place at 1040°F (560°C), without holding the temperature. Anneal/soak the vase at 970°F (520°C) for 15 minutes.

Photo 117
Colorful stippled squares

Photo 118
Detail of design

PROJECT 9 – CHAMPAGNE GLASSES

110

MATERIALS	COLORS
Champagne glasses (two)	
Opaque paint	Black
Transparent paint	Yellow
Transparent paint	Purple
Painting medium	
Painting medium thinner	
Outline medium	
Fine sponge	
Clear adhesive film	

It's most unusual to be able to celebrate special occasions by toasting with champagne glasses you've decorated yourself. What's more, these glasses will gradually become desirable pieces to collectors. The most pleasant aspect of this fact is that the pieces will have come from your own workshop.

Draw a pencil line around the glass to designate the border of the pen-worked area. Again with a pencil, sketch the pattern onto the glass surface. (You may draw your sketch on paper and then apply this to the inside of the glass instead.) Then draw the design with a pen, as described in the pen-work section on page 72. Practiced painters can complete this step freehand, without a tracing or pattern. Fire the glasses to 1040°F (560°C) using side heat.

Protect the decorated areas with clear adhesive film. Stipple the rest of one glass with yellow and the rest of the other with purple. Then fire a second time to 1040°F (560°C), again with side heat.

Add the shaded, colored motifs and fire the glasses a third time to 1040°F (560°C) with side heat.

Add bright gold or bright platinum accents to the rims and to the decorated portions of the glasses. After you've signed the glasses, fire them a fourth and final time to 1040°F (560°C) with side heat.

Photo 119
Champagne glasses

112

Photos 120 and 121
Glasses with pen-drawn designs

Photos 122 and 123
Stippled glasses

114

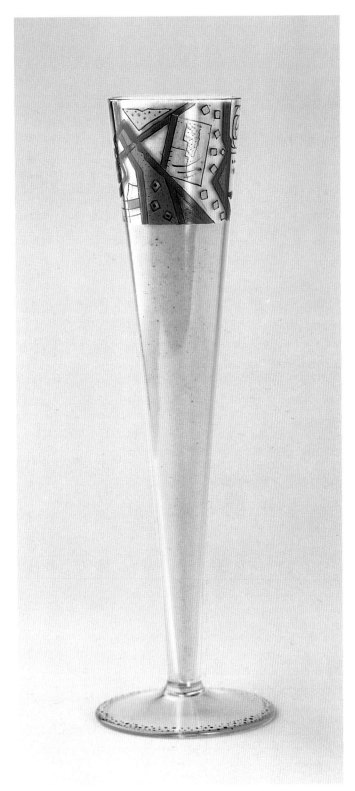

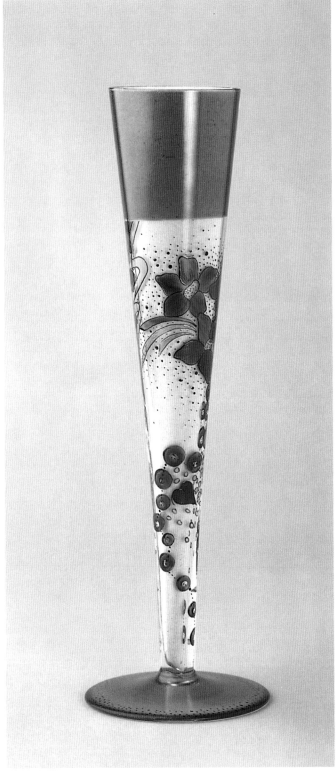

Photos 124 and 125
Glasses with added colors

PROJECT 10 – SLENDER VASE

MATERIALS	COLORS
Glass vase	
Satin matte paint	White
Opaque paint	Black
Opaque paint	White
Opaque paint	Red
Bright platinum	
Liquid resist (decal covercoat)	
Painting medium	
Painting medium thinner	
Outline medium	

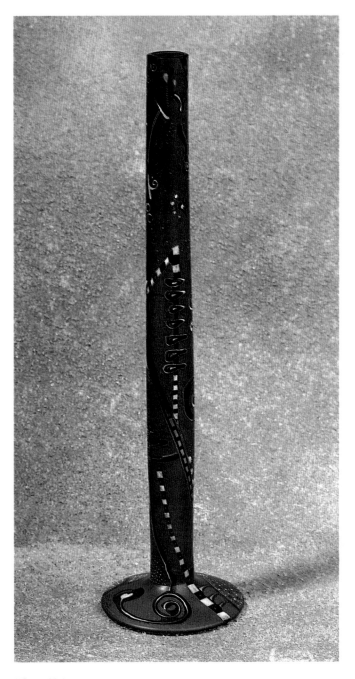

Photo 126
Slender vase

116   This unusually shaped vase demands a fitting decoration. In the design shown here, I've used dark decoration to lend the piece a certain weight and festiveness, which in turn provides an interesting contrast to the slender shape. An entirely different design could have been used instead.

Stipple the entire vase with a mixture of one part black and one part satin matte. Fire it to 1040°F (560°C) with side heat. The vase will take on a semimatte anthracite surface. In the second step, cover the vase with a generous spiral of clear adhesive film. Then apply liquid resist freehand to the uncovered areas to make imaginative patterns. When the liquid resist is dry, stipple the entire vase with white satin matte. Remove the film and the dried resist, check the piece for irregularities, and using side heat, fire it a second time to 1040°F (560°F).

Then mix the opaque white and opaque red paints—separately—with outline medium and use a pen to draw designs onto the sections that were covered with liquid resist. Add a delicate bright platinum design to the spiral. Sign the vase and using side heat, fire it a final time to 1040°F (560°C).

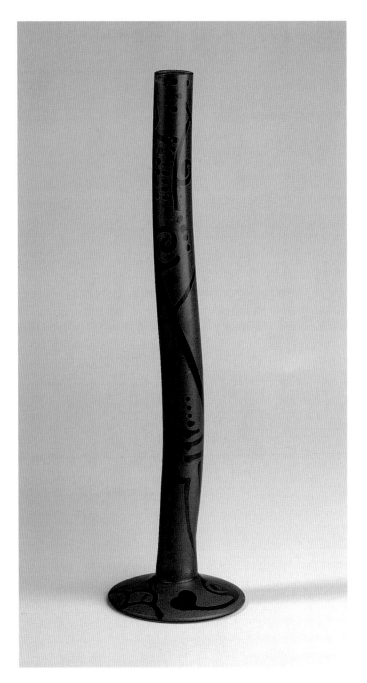

Photo 127
The vase after the second firing

PROJECT 11 – FLOWER VASE

Photo 128
Flower vase

118

MATERIALS	COLORS
Vase (glass)	
Satin matte paint	White
Opaque paint	White
Luster	Yellow
Luster	Bright green
Luster	Carmine
Luster	Blue
Bright gold	
Liquid resist (decal covercoat)	
Painting medium	
Painting medium thinner	
Luster thinner	
Clear adhesive film	
Fine sponge	

A late summer's evening inspired the design on this flower vase. The leaves are gradually beginning to fade, and fog is spreading over the countryside.

Coat the upper two-thirds of the vase with clear adhesive film. Use a waterproof felt-tip pen to draw the leaves on it. Then use a craft knife to cut out the leaves and pull them off. Remove the adhesive film from the bottom portion of the vase as well. Clean the vase with mineral spirits and stipple it with satin matte. On the bottom portion, use a wipe-out stick to create a freeform design in the wet satin matte. Fire the vase to 1040°F (560°C) with side heat.

Protect the bottom portion of the vase, up to the line formed by the lowest leaves, with clear adhesive film. Add nicely shaded lusters to some of the leaves and carefully fill in the other leaves with just one luster, so that some leaves are shaded and others are solid. Remove the film and fire a second time to 1040°F (560°C) with side heat.

Cover the bottom part of the vase with clear adhesive film again. Cut out the same leaf motifs as those on the upper part of the vase. Then stipple these leaves with satin matte and white paint, mixed in a ratio of 1:1. Outline the brightly colored leaves with bright gold. I also applied bright gold to some of the spaces between the leaves. Sign the vase and fire it a final time to 1040°F (560°C). Soak the piece for 20 minutes at 970°F (520°C).

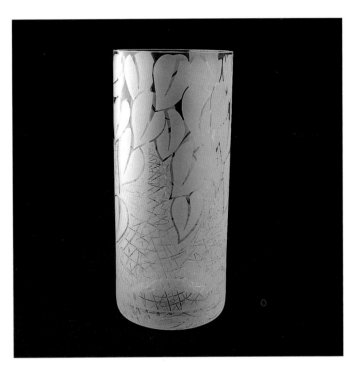

Photo 129
Flower vase with a white satin matte background

Photo 130
Leaves painted with lusters

PROJECT 12 – ROUND VASE

120

The round shape of this vase encouraged me to decorate it with round motifs. The fresh yellow brings a first breath of spring into the house.

First, stipple the surface of the round vase with satin matte. Fire the vase, using two-thirds side heat and one-third top heat, to 1040°F (560°C).

MATERIALS	COLORS
Glass vase	
Satin matte paint	White
Luster	Yellow
Luster	Carmine
Luster	Violet
Opaque paint	Black
Relief paint	White
Bright gold	
Painting medium	
Painting medium thinner	
Crystal ice, fine	
Adhesive for crystal ice	
Fine sponge	

Prepare a luster bath containing yellow, carmine, and violet, adding more yellow than the other two colors. Be careful to follow the instructions on page 80 when doing this. Dip the vase in the luster bath, and then fire it a second time at 1040°F (560°C), with two-thirds side heat and one-third top heat. Next, outline several of the dipped colors with fine lines of crystal ice adhesive. Also paint round motifs with the adhesive. Sprinkle fine crystal ice over the adhesive. When the adhesive is dry, check the vase for excess bits of crystal ice. Then, using opaque black, trace more of the dip outlines with a brush and add generous motifs. A third firing follows at 1040°F (560°C), with two-thirds side heat and one-third top heat.

Underscore the details with white relief and bright gold. Decorate the crystal ice with bright gold as well. Use yellow luster to make the final touches. Sign your vase and fire it one last time to 1040°F (560°C), using two-thirds side heat and one-third top heat.

Photo 131
Round vase after third firing

Photo 132
Round vase

PROJECT 13 – GLASS DISH

122

This glass dish is an unusual object, one which will look even more tempting when it's filled with candies and set on a table. With its curved shape and contrasting decoration, it certainly isn't your run-of-the-mill project.

Using a pencil, draw a band along the outer edge of the dish. Then fill in this band with fine roses and leaves. To make the roses, draw both sides of your brush through the opaque beige red and one side through the dark red, as described on page 73. Then draw a ball shape with a round upward movement.

MATERIALS	COLORS
Glass dish	
Satin matte paint	White
Opaque paint	Beige-red
Opaque paint	Dark red
Opaque paint	Yellow green
Opaque paint	Dark green
Opaque paint	Black
Relief paint	White
Luster	Green
Bright gold	
Painting medium	
Painting medium thinner	
Luster thinner	
Clear adhesive film	

Shade the focal points of the rose petals with dark red and add two petals on each side. Then, with the tip of a clean brush, draw the outline of each blossom. Create the leaves in a similar fashion. Apply yellow green to both sides of the brush and dark green to the tip. Then form the leaf using corresponding movements in the shape of the letter C. When the paint is dry or after firing it at 1040°F (560°C), draw the outlines of the roses and the leaves very finely with black. Apply small dots of white relief to the background of the band. Fire the glass dish at 1040°F (560°C) with top heat.

Next, cut out neat spirals of clear adhesive film and transfer them onto the undecorated areas of the glass dish. Protect the rim of flowers with film, then stipple the dish delicately with satin matte. Remove the film and, using top heat, fire the piece again to 1040°F (560°F). For this firing, place the dish in the kiln with its opening face down.

Protect the band of roses with clear adhesive film again. Then stipple the glass dish with green luster diluted in a ratio of 1:1 with luster thinner. Allow the luster to dry well and then draw a fine bright gold design on both sides of the rose band. Finally, sign the piece and fire it a last time to 1040°F (560°C), using top heat.

Photo 133
Glass dish

124

Photo 134
Rim decorated with roses

Photo 135
Stippled background

PROJECT 14 – WALL MIRROR

Is it a wall mirror or a picture? Enjoy this unusual project, which you can make in colors that complement your decor.

Stipple the entire glass pane with white satin matte and fire it to 1040°F (560°C) with top heat. Then paint on the decal paper, using opaque sky blue and opaque dark blue. Add a little opaque yellow in several places. Cover the designs with decal covercoat. When the covercoat has dried, cut or tear sections from the decal. Next, apply the decals to the glass, reserving an area for the mirror. If necessary, read the section on page 86 about using decals. Be careful that no bubbles form under the decals. If they do, pierce them with a needle, and press any water out. When the decals are securely attached to the piece, apply coarse crystal ice to various areas. Fire the piece a second time, using top heat, to 1040°F (560°C).

Decorate a portion of the crystal ice with bright platinum. Use a pen to add bright platinum and opaque yellow accents. Sign the piece and fire it one more time to 1040°F (560°C) with top heat.

Trace the area that you've reserved for the mirror. Transfer this pattern onto the mirror, cut out the mirror freehand, and grind its edges very carefully. Attach the mirror to the reserved area with strong double-sided tape. Attach a hanger, also using double-sided tape, onto the back surface.

MATERIALS	COLORS	DIMENSIONS
Sheet of glass Mirror		16" x 16" (40 x 40 cm) 6" x 12" (15 x 30 cm)
Satin matte paint Opaque paint Opaque paint Opaque paint Bright platinum	White Dark blue Sky blue Yellow	
Crystal ice, course		
Adhesive for crystal ice		
Painting medium		
Painting medium thinner		
Decal medium		
Decal paper		
Decal covercoat		
Fine sponge		

Photo 136
Fired decal

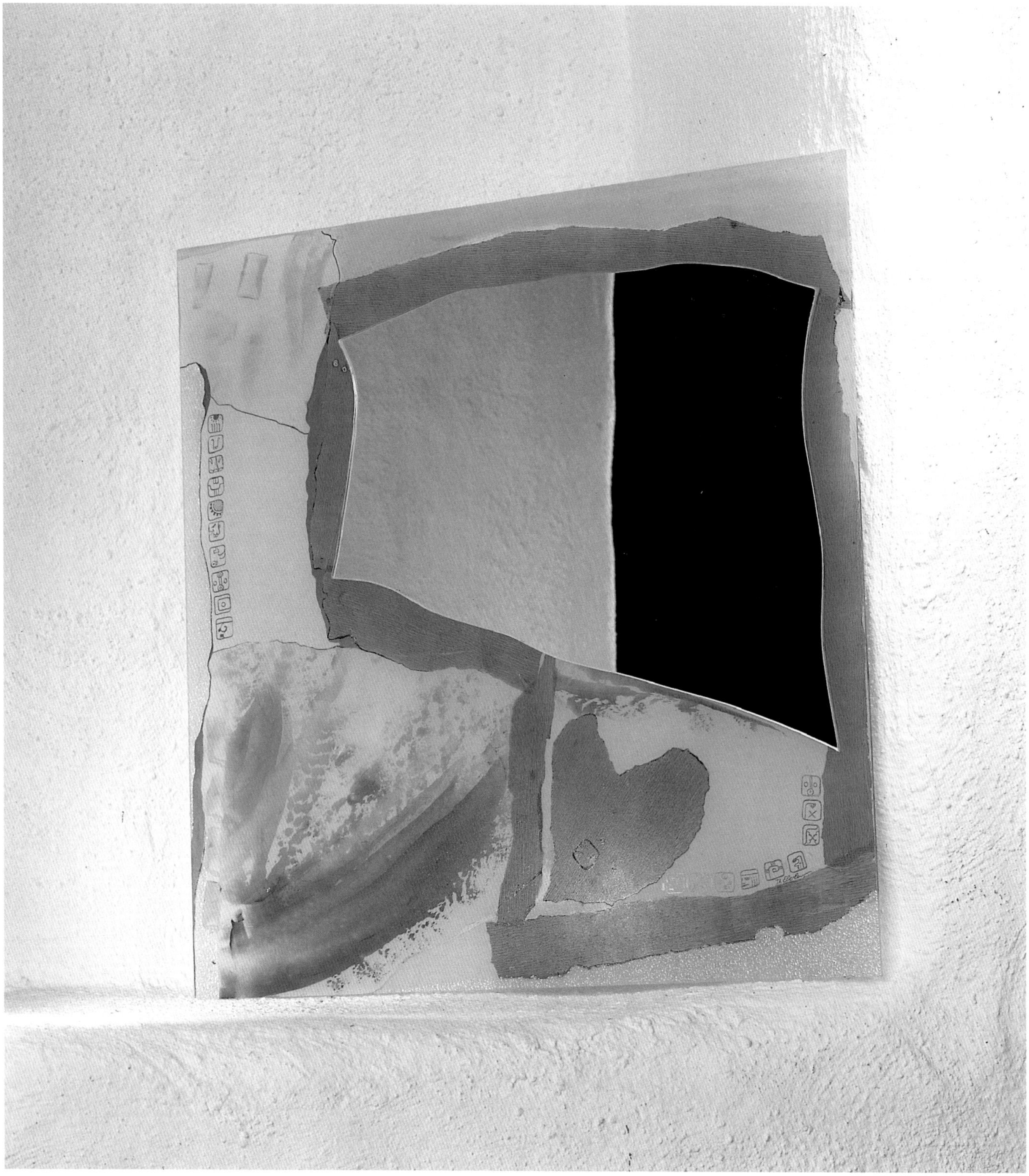

126

Photo 137
Wall mirror

PROJECT 15 – BOWL WITH AZTEC CALENDAR

This lavish project is more suited for practiced painters. The Aztec calendar and the simple shape of the bowl inspired me to create this composition. Earthy colors are wonderfully suitable.

Cut twenty-one squares of clear adhesive film. Center them on the bowl. Stipple the bowl, excluding the bottom, with metallic copper. Remove the film and complete the first firing at 1040°F (560°C) with side heat. Soak at this temperature for 10 minutes.

The symbols of the Aztec calendar are painted in the squares with a short, thick brush. This is easier if you paste a sketch of the designs on the inside of the bowl. When the colors are dry, use a fine brush or pen to outline every motif in black. If you wish, you can simplify making these outlines by firing the bowl again before drawing them. The second firing is again at 1040°F (560°F) and the temperature is not held.

MATERIALS	COLORS
Glass bowl	
Metallic paint	Copper
Opaque paint	Dark green
Opaque paint	Dark blue
Opaque paint	Black
Opaque paint	Bright red
Opaque paint	Red
Opaque paint	Light ivory
Opaque paint	Red brown
Opaque paint	Dark brown
Transparent paint	Yellow
Bright gold	
Painting medium	
Painting medium thinner	
Outline medium	
Clear adhesive film	

Photo 138
Bowl stippled with metallic copper

128

Photo 139
Bowl with Aztec calendar

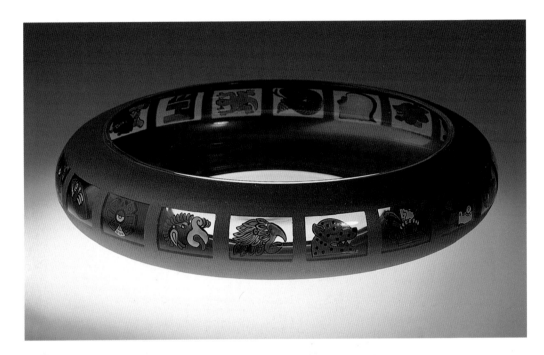

Photo 140
Painted and outlined motifs

Use clear adhesive film to protect the outer edges of each square on the inside of the bowl. Using bright gold, draw the outline of each square on the outside of the bowl. Stipple every area on the inside with transparent yellow. Remove the film. With a pen, record the day and meaning of each individual symbol underneath the corresponding area on the inside of the bowl. Check your work and sign it. The final firing is at 1040°F (560°C); this temperature is not held.

Photo 141
Detail of the bowl

PROJECT 16 – DEEP BOWL

130

Venetian masks and the happy mood of a carnival inspired me to make this colorful bowl. The stylized faces remind me of the figures at an Italian carnival, and the warm orange color suggests the sensual atmosphere.

On the outside of the bowl, use a waterproof felt-tip pen to draw the mask motifs, the band across the bowl, and the very narrow rim. Then, on the inside of the bowl, use a wipe-out stick and black relief paint to trace these pen lines. (This bowl is painted on the inside.) Cover the background behind the masks with dots of black relief. Stipple the outer rim with red. Check the piece for mistakes and fire it at 1040°F (560°C) with top heat.

MATERIALS	COLORS
Glass bowl	
Satin matte paint	White
Relief paint	Black
Opaque paint	Light red
Transparent paint	Green
Transparent paint	Yellow
Transparent paint	Blue
Opaque paint	Red
Bright gold	
Painting medium	
Painting medium thinner	
Outline medium	
Liquid resist (decal covercoat)	
Clear adhesive film	

Photo 142
Bowl outlined with relief black

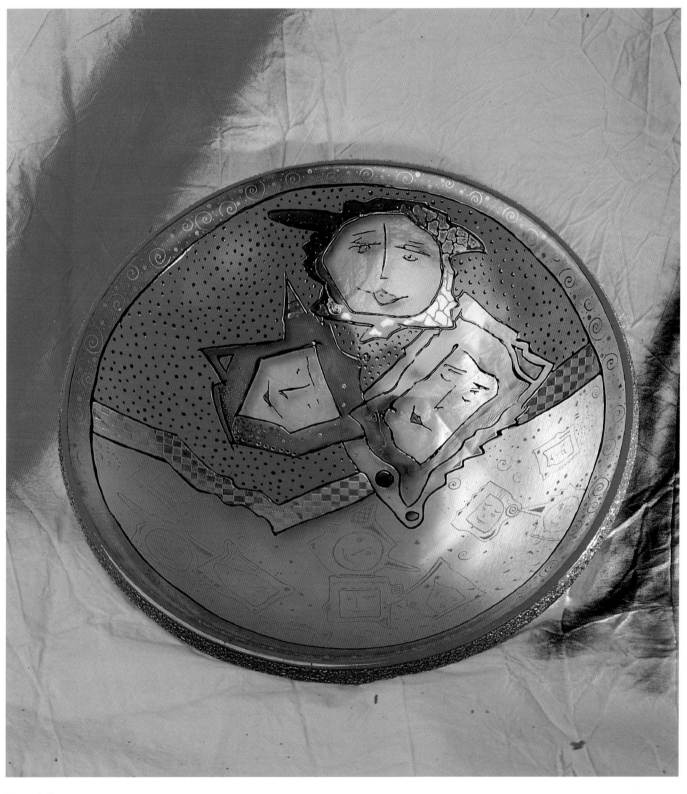

Photo 143
Deep bowl

132   Protect the masks with a thick application of liquid resist, as described on page 85, and allow the resist to dry. Then stipple the mask background with light red and the other part of the background with opaque red and satin matte mixed in a ratio of 1:1. Remove the dried resist with a pointed object and fire the bowl again, using top heat, at 1040°F (560°C).

Cover the band that runs diagonally across the bowl with small squares of clear adhesive film. Then stipple the band with white satin matte. Remove the adhesive resist. Mix the bright red with outline medium, and draw the smaller mask designs onto the lighter portion of the bowl. Fire the piece again at 1040°F (560°C) with top heat.

Paint the mask's bright colors with very diluted paint. Stipple the wide band with paint as well. Fire the bowl at 1040°F (560°C) with top heat. Next, use bright gold to draw the small details on the masks and to decorate the satin matte squares running diagonally across the bowl. Also gild the wide rim with delicate motifs. Apply coarse crystal ice onto the outer edge of the bowl. Sign and check the piece before firing it a final time at 1040°F (560°C) with top heat. Because of the bowl's thickness, with each firing, you must anneal/soak the piece for 20 minutes at 970°F (520°C).

Photo 144
Bowl with painted and decorated background

Photo 145
Detail of the bowl

PROJECT 17 – PICTURE

MATERIALS	COLORS	DIMENSIONS
Window glass		12" x 12" (30 x 30 cm)
Window glass		17-1/2" x 17-1/2" (44 x 44 cm)
Satin matte paint	White	
Opaque paint	Dark red	
Opaque paint	Black	
Opaque paint	Dark green	
Opaque paint	Bright green	
Opaque paint	Lemon yellow	
Opaque paint	Silver	
Opaque paint	Silver iris	
Metallic paint		
Luster		
Liquid resist (decal covercoat)		
Painting medium		
Painting medium thinner		
Luster thinner		
Clear adhesive film		
Sponge		

A glass painting like this one doesn't necessarily have to have a special use, but can simply be an artistically designed object that brings us pleasure. The lotus bud appears even lovelier when delicately framed. Similar to a scene viewed through a lace curtain, this is a picture that can enhance any room.

Draw the bud on a piece of paper. On both the front and back sides of a 12" x 12" (30 x 30 cm) window-glass pane, use clear adhesive film to cover a centered border, 5/8" (1.5 cm) wide, around a 5-1/2" x 5-1/2" (14 x 14 cm) square. Then lay your sketch under the pane and paint the bud onto the glass, using delicate shadowing. Outline all the blossom leaves, and paint them with graduated shades of green and red. Then decorate the back surface of the pane. Lay the glass on four felt coasters to protect the painted front surface. Stipple the outermost border of the back surface with the bud colors, using nice shading. Stipple the back side of the bud with metallic silver. Then remove all the pieces of clear adhesive film and check the piece. Stipple a 17-1/2" x 17-1/2" (44 x 44 cm) background pane with satin matte; this will serve as the frame. Then fire both pieces for the first time at 1040°F (560°C) with top heat. When doing this, take care that the pane with the bud painted on it rests in the kiln with the bud facing up and that it is supported underneath—on its unpainted surfaces—with pieces of a ceramic fiber sheet, so that no ugly marks result on the painted surfaces.

134

Photo 146
Picture

Cover the bud and its square background with narrow strips of clear adhesive film. Along the narrow border of this square, cut small diamonds in the film. Apply a variety of liquid resist designs to the outermost border. Then float silver iris luster onto the bud and its square background (see page 80) and stipple the outer border with satin matte. Remove every other square in the narrow, diamond print border and use a brush to paint these red. Remove the liquid resist and the adhesive film with a craft knife. After you've signed the picture, check it carefully.

On the back surface of the background piece, use clear adhesive film to cover a 3-1/8"-wide (8 cm) border with a pattern of squares. Remove every other square and stipple the border with metallic silver. Then fire the panes a second time at 1040°F (560°C) with top heat. Support the two panes on small pieces of ceramic fiber sheet to protect the painted surfaces.

Use double-sided transparent tape to mount the picture with the bud in the center of the background pane. Attach a hanger on the back surface with extra-strong double-sided tape.

Photo 147
Picture after the first firing

Photo 148
Picture after the second firing

Lampwork

Important Information

As already mentioned in the introduction, lampwork can be done with a multipurpose torch. Because the flame isn't as hot as the flame from a mixture of propane and oxygen, possibilities for designs are a little limited. Nevertheless, we can still make very nice projects if we use our imaginations and have good ideas.

The rule regarding coefficients of expansion also applies to lampwork: You must not melt together glass of different expansion coefficients (see page 26). In addition, you must be careful never to heat up the glass quickly when you're doing lampwork; always heat it slowly. Don't hold the glass rod in the center of the flame for any great length of time; instead, approach the middle of the flame slowly, using circular motions.

I often use remnants of Bullseye glass for lampwork. Because this readily available glass has already been tested for compatibility, you can be sure that you won't be faced with any unpleasant surprises. Cut the remnants in strips approximately 1/4" (5 mm) wide. You can make lovely glass beads from these and can decorate them by adding stringers (or threads).

Working with a multipurpose torch is a lot of fun and is also a very playful activity, but for good results, you'll need a little practice. Don't give up too quickly. Remember that the pieces you make with a torch can also be painted.

Equipment and Materials

Photo 149
1. *Multipurpose torch with a hard solder burner*
2. *Bead separator*
3. *Vermiculite (annealing granules) in a tin can*
4. *Heat-resistant ceramic fiberboard pad*
5. *Stainless steel mandrels*
6. *Decorating tools*
7. *Protective glasses (good sunglasses)*
8. *Large glass filled with sand*
9. *Glass rods, glass strips, stringers (or threads), etc.*

Required Materials for Lampwork with a Multipurpose Soldering Torch

❱ *Multipurpose Soldering Torch*

The multipurpose soldering torch with a hard solder burner runs on butane gas, canisters of which are available in a variety of stores, including camping stores. A new canister of gas always has the greatest pressure, so if you plan to make several projects one after the other, always begin with the largest project, because the higher initial pressure produces a hotter flame.

❱ *Bead Separator*

When you make beads, you'll need to apply this special separating agent to the stainless steel rods (or mandrels) in order to prevent the glass from sticking to them. The powdered separator is mixed with water to form a thick mixture into which the rods—roughened with fine sandpaper—are dipped. To dry the dipped rods, stick them upright into a sand-filled glass.

❯ *Vermiculite*

Vermiculite granules, which serve as an excellent insulating material, are used to cool and anneal hot beads. You'll bury the beads, while they're still on the steel mandrels, in the vermiculite for 20 to 60 minutes. (The amount of time required will depend on the size of the beads.) The vermiculite will prevent the beads from cooling down too quickly; rapid cooling can cause stress and breakage.

❯ *Ceramic Fiberboard Pad*

A piece of old fiberboard, 1" (2.5 cm) thick, serves very well as a work surface. While a normal work surface is easily burned, this material won't suffer if you absentmindedly place hot materials on it or if a drop of molten glass falls from a rod.

❯ *Stainless Steel Mandrels*

Steel mandrels (or rods) of various thicknesses, dipped into bead separator, are the tools around which you'll wrap the hot glass in order to shape it into beads. The mandrel creates a hole within each bead.

❯ *Decorating Tools*

Long tweezers, tongs with flat tips, a carbon paddle, small graphite plates, and graphite reamers—these are the tools you'll need for lampwork. With the tweezers, for example, you can pull small bits off the soft glass. The flat tongs serve to flatten the glass. The exact functions of these tools will be explained in connection with the projects in which they're used.

❯ *Protective Glasses*

A good pair of protective glasses or polaroid sunglasses are a good protection against the bright light of the flame. Make it a habit to wear these glasses whenever you work with a torch.

❯ *Container of Sand*

The simplest way to keep mandrels handy is to place them upright in a sand-filled container.

❯ *Glass Rods and Strips*

The basic materials for making beads and glass planter ornaments (two of the projects we'll cover in this section) are a variety of glass rods, glass cut into strips, and stringers (or threads). You can also reshape ordinary drinking glasses by using a torch. A wine glass with a small nick in its rim can be transformed with a torch into a funny object.

Correct Procedures

140

Prepare your work space carefully before beginning. Lay out all your tools so they're ready to use and place your prepared mandrels in the container of sand. Check the torch. Is it properly closed? Do you have enough butane available? Select glass rods or pieces of glass and clean them thoroughly. Put on your protective glasses. Now you can begin this fascinating work. Turn on the flame of the burner completely. (Follow the manufacturer's instructions exactly.) The flame should be slightly blue in color. Its inner portion, which is especially hot, will be a more intense blue.

First warm the glass in the outer part of the flame, turning it continuously as you do. In principle, the glass should always be kept in motion while it's in the flame or it may overheat and melt. Only when the glass is well warmed and begins to lose its color should you approach the hot center of the flame.

Lampwork Projects

PROJECT 1 – GLASS BEADS

To make glass beads, take the prepared mandrel in your left hand and the glass rod in your right. Then warm the upper portions of both the mandrel and glass rod in the flame, turning the pieces continuously. When the rod changes color, move it into the hot part of the flame. It will first turn dark red and will then become brighter until it is orange. At this point, the glass will be soft and the mandrel hot; you can begin using a turning motion to start wrapping the glass around the mandrel.

When the bead is the desired size, pull the glass rod slowly away from the mandrel and melt away the thin threads of glass to separate the glass rod from the bead. Remember to keep rotating the mandrel and the bead that is on it while holding them in the flame. Now decorate the bead with stringers (or threads) or change its shape by pressing the glass with tongs. Photo 150 shows you several examples of bead designs.

After the beads have cooled and annealed in the vermiculite, remove them from the mandrels with a slight twisting motion.

Photo 150
Decoration possibilities for beads

Photo 151
Making beads

Photo 152
Burning through the glass thread

Photo 153
Glass bead jewelry

PROJECT 2 – PLANTER ORNAMENTS

144   Grasp a long glass rod with both hands, one at each end, and warm it by holding the middle portion in the upper part of the flame. Remember to keep rotating the rod. After a short time, move the glass into the hot part of the flame. Turn the rod until it is orange and then press its ends slightly towards its center. A thickening will result in the middle of the rod.

Melt off one of the portions of the rod that extends from the thickened area. Now flatten the thickened area with tongs and bend it forward slightly. Using tweezers, you can pull some small bits of the soft glass outward.

Vermiculite isn't sufficient for annealing projects of this size, so when the planter ornament is finished, place it in a kiln and fire it to 970°F (520°C). Soak at that temperature for 20 minutes. Then let the closed kiln cool to room temperature.

I also decorated my planter ornaments with paint and bright gold.

Photo 154
Thickening the glass rod

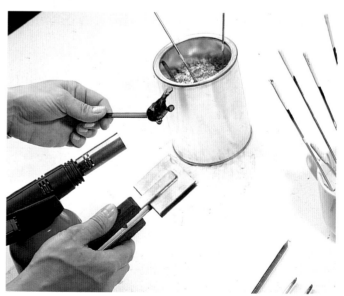

Photo 155
Shaping the planter ornaments

Photo 156
Planter ornaments

PROJECT 3 – RESHAPING DRINKING GLASSES

146

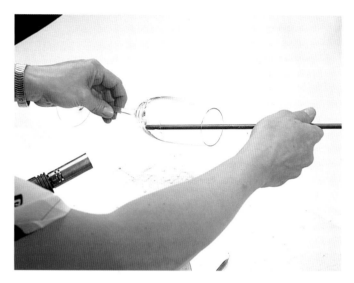

Photo 157
Reshaping the glass

Reshaping old drinking glasses can make them attractive, and these modified glasses will also make very unusual and special gifts. In addition, you can mend old glasses with damaged rims while giving them an attractive, new look.

To warm the glass up, turn it while holding it in the outer part of the flame. Then progress slowly to the hot part of the flame and soften the part of the glass that you want to reshape. One way to create a new shape is by using a carbon paddle to press the soft glass in at a right angle. Try using tweezers to reshape the edge of the upper rim.

To distort the stem of a wine glass, grasp the glass by the bowl, hold the base over the flame, and shape the glass when it's soft.

Allow your imagination to run free. When you're satisfied with the result, you must anneal the glass. Place it in the kiln and fire it to 970°F (520°C). Soak at that temperature for 15 minutes; then allow the kiln to cool to room temperature.

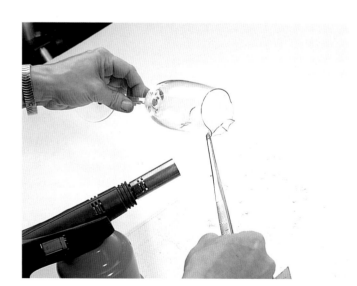

Photo 158
Reshaping the rim

Photo 159
Reshaping the stem

Photo 160
Reshaped glass

Troubleshooting

Glass Fusing

The edges of your fused glass aren't nicely rounded.

You didn't fire the piece to sufficiently high temperatures. Repeat the firing at a temperature 40°F (20°C) higher than that of the previous firing.

Dull spots appear on the glass.

You've heated up the glass too slowly at the higher temperature level or have held the temperature too long. In full-fuse firing, you must complete the rapid heating phase quickly. One solution is to fire at a temperature 20°F (10°C) higher instead of holding the temperature.

A residue of shelf primer remains on the piece.

You loaded the kiln before the shelf primer was dry.

Glass Painting

After firing, the paints aren't glossy.

Take note of the firing curve; perhaps you didn't fire at a high enough temperature.

The drinking glasses bend during firing.

Drinking glasses must be fired using side heat. If a temperature of 1040°F (560°C) is too high for your kiln, reduce the temperature by 40°F (20°C) and hold the final temperature for 5 minutes.

How can you rescue bent drinking glasses?

You can often reshape bent drinking glasses by hanging them by their bases in the kiln and firing them at a temperature 40°F (20°C) higher, that is at a temperature of 1080°F (580°C).

Paint won't flow from your pen.

Re-mix the paint with outline medium and add several drops of water. If your surroundings are very warm, it's advisable to add water to the paint.

You can't remove all the liquid resist (decal overcoat).

You applied too thin a coat. Allow the paint to dry completely and apply more resist to the same areas. When the added resist has dried, you should be able to remove it effortlessly.

Your stippling doesn't look even.

The paint is too thick. Remove the entire stippled application, add more thinner to the paint, and stipple the piece again. Now your stippling should be successful.

Your luster won't form a film on the surface of the water.

The water is too cold; change it.

Only a portion of the piece is fired correctly.

Have your kiln checked by an expert. It's possible that the heating elements aren't heating evenly. Make sure that there's sufficient air space between the parts of the kiln when outfitting it. The hot air must circulate well and must be able to reach every part of the object being fired.

You need to remove traces of bright gold, bright platinum, or luster from your glass.

Use a strong rust remover (from a hardware or drug store). To protect your skin, always wear rubber gloves when handling this substance; rust remover is very corrosive. Rinse the cleaned glass areas with clear water.

Lampwork

The glass rods won't soften.

The pressure is too low. Replace the butane canister with a new one.

The beads turn out matte.

You worked too long in the hottest (bluest) part of the flame.

You have trouble removing the bead separator from the insides of the beads.

Use a toothpick to force steel wool through the openings.

Resources

U.S.A.

American Crafts Council
40 West 53rd Street
New York, NY 14830

The Glass Art Society Inc.
PO Box 1364
Corning, NY 14830

The Stained Glass Association of America
4050 Broadway, Suite 219
Kansas City, MO 64111

INTERNATIONAL

Artists in Stained Glass (AISG) Canada
c/o Ontario Crafts Council
35 McCaul Street
Toronto M5T 1V7

British Artists in Glass
c/o Broadfield House Glass Museum
Barnett Lane, Kingswinford
West Midlands DY6 9QA, U.K.

British Society of Master Glass Painters
11 Landsdowne Road, Muswell Hill
London N10 2AX, U.K.

The Canadian Crafts Council
46 Elgin Street, Suite 16
Ottawa, Canada K1P 5K6

The Crafts Council
44A Pentonville Road
London N1 9BY, U.K.

The Crafts Council of Australia
100 George Street
Sydney, New South Wales 2000, Australia

Crafts Council of Japan
503 Yoyogi 4-28-8
Shibuya-Ku
Tokyo 151, Japan

Crafts Council of New Zealand
22 The Terrace, PO Box 498
Wellington 1, New Zealand

Districts de l'Exempio Adjunctament de Barcelona
Casa Elizaldo
Valencia 302, Spain

The Glass Association
Broadfield House, Glass Museum
Barnett Lane, Kingswinford
West Midlands DY6 9QA, U.K.

INT Nat. De Nouvel Objet Visuel
27 Rue de l'Universite
F75007 Paris, France

Suggested Reading

Bray, Charles.
> *The Dictionary of Glass: Materials and Techniques.*
> Philadelphia: University of Pennsylvania Press, 1965.
> (London: A&C Black; Australia: Craftsman House)

Cummings, Keith.
> *Techniques of Kiln-Formed Glass.*
> Ouiedo, Florida: Axner Co., Inc., 1997.
> (London: A&C Black; Australia, Craftsman House)

Fraser, Harry.
> *The Electric Kiln, A User's Manual.*
> Ouiedo, Florida: Axner Co., Inc., 1995.
> (London: A&C Black; Australia, Craftsman House)

Rossol, Monona.
> *The Artist's Complete Health and Safety Guide.* 2nd ed.
> New York: Allworth Press, 1994.

Acknowledgments

Lark Books wishes to thank the author, Bettina Eberle, for her patience, her exceptional language skills, and her sense of humor. We are also deeply grateful for the advice provided by the following people:

Mr. Edward W. Hoy (chairman)
Ed Hoy's International
Naperville, Illinois, U.S.A.

Mr. Gene Messick
Lightworks Studio
Earl, North Carolina, U.S.A.

Mr. Jon C. Rarick, (president)
Mr. Eric Wagg (lab manager)
Reusche & Co.
TransWorld Supplies, Inc.
Greeley, Colorado, U.S.A.

Index